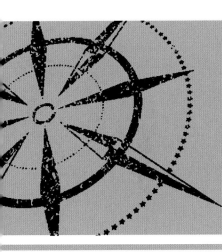

MAMMALS OF THE
NORTHERN HEMISPHERE

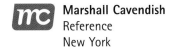 **Marshall Cavendish**
Reference
New York

Marshall Cavendish

Copyright © 2011 Marshall Cavendish Corporation

Published by Marshall Cavendish Reference

An imprint of Marshall Cavendish Corporation

Website: www.marshallcavendish.us

This publication represents the opinions and views of the
authors based on personal experience, knowledge, and
research. The information in this book serves as a general
guide only. The author and publisher have used their best
efforts in preparing this book and disclaim liability rising
directly and indirectly from the use and application of this
book.

Other Marshall Cavendish Offices:

Marshall Cavendish International (Asia) Private Limited, 1
New Industrial Road, Singapore 536196 • Marshall Cavendish
International (Thailand) Co Ltd. 253 Asoke, 12th Flr,
Sukhumvit 21 Road, Klongtoey Nua, Wattana, Bangkok
10110, Thailand • Marshall Cavendish (Malaysia) Sdn Bhd,
Times Subang, Lot 46, Subang Hi-Tech Industrial Park, Batu
Tiga, 40000 Shah Alam, Selangor Darul Ehsan, Malaysia

Marshall Cavendish is a trademark of Times Publishing
Limited

All websites were available and accurate when this book was
sent to press.

Library of Congress Cataloging-in-Publication Data
Mammals of the Northern Hemisphere.

    p. cm.

  Includes index.

  ISBN 978-0-7614-7936-9

  1. Mammals--Northern Hemisphere--Juvenile literature. I.
Marshall

Cavendish Reference.

  QL706.2.M285 2010

  599.09181'3--dc22

2010006398

Printed in Malaysia

14 13 12 11 10 1 2 3 4 5

MARSHALL CAVENDISH

Publisher: Paul Bernabeo

Production Manager: Mike Esposito

THE BROWN REFERENCE GROUP PCL

Managing Editor: Tim Harris

Designer: Lynne Lennon

Picture Researcher: Laila Torsun

Indexer: Ann Barrett

Design Manager: David Poole

Editorial Director: Lindsey Lowe

FOREWORD

Humans have been keen observers of mammals for millennia. Archeological sites in Europe preserve evidence that members of our species, *Homo sapiens*, made close observations of the anatomy and behavior of other mammals more than 30,000 years ago. The extensive galleries of rock art at these sites attest to the intimate knowledge that those artists had of their local mammal communities. Over the past 10,000 years, with the spread of human agriculture and the development of increasingly urbanized societies, people have domesticated several kinds of mammals, and this has fed our knowledge of comparative mammalian biology. Over 2,000 years ago, the Greek philosopher Aristotle laid the foundations for the scientific study of mammals, and we derive our knowledge of the mammals alive on Earth today from a long lineage of subsequent mammalogists.

Here in the early years of the 21st century, 5,421 species of mammals have been officially named and recognized, and about 25 new species of mammals are named each year. Most of the new mammal species are small-bodied and nocturnal forms of shrew, rodent, and bat; however, larger-bodied species have also been described in recent years, including new primates, deer, and even whales. In addition to the discovery of new mammal species, we also continue to discover new facts about familiar species, and our discoveries are made at an increasingly rapid pace.

This book will introduce readers to current knowledge of selected mammals of the Northern Hemisphere, from beavers to bears and killer whales. The entries are carefully and beautifully illustrated, and this book, along with its companion volume on the mammals of the Southern Hemisphere, provides an excellent resource for young students of mammalogy, as well as anyone curious about the lives of our closest relatives.

The entries are drawn from *Exploring Mammals*, an inspired 20-volume collection that covered almost all of the world's living mammal lineages. Each of the entries provides basic natural history information related to anatomy, locomotion, diet, habitat, social life, reproductive behavior, conservation status, and more. There is such a wealth of knowledge in these books that even experienced mammalogists will discover valuable new information.

Alan Shabel

Alan Shabel is a professor in the Department of Integrative Biology at the University of Berkeley, California, who specializes in mammalogy.

Additional related information is available in the 20-volume *Exploring Mammals* and the corresponding online *Exploring Mammals* database at www.marshallcavendishdigital.com.

INTRODUCTION

Each article in *Mammals of the Northern Hemisphere* concentrates on a particular mammal or group of mammals. Each is illustrated with photographs and labeled diagrams and covers the following main features: profile, anatomy, habitat, behavior, and survival.

PROFILE provides an introductory portrait of the animal, the different species that exist, and describes its close relatives and ancestors. The special boxed features in this section include:

• **Key facts**—a concise description of the mammal's common and scientific names, its subspecies if appropriate, and the habitat, range, and appearance of the mammal.

• **Relatives**—this box provides an illustrated summary of some of the animal's closest relatives.

• **Did you know? Ancestors**—a thorough description of the mammal's ancestors.

ANATOMY describes what the mammal looks like inside and out. It includes a large annotated artwork of the mammal and information about its skeleton, skull, and teeth. The boxed feature in the anatomy section is a

• **Fact file**—an in-depth examination of the size and coloration of each mammal, with precise lengths, heights, and weights.

HABITAT describes the place where the animal naturally lives, with a map showing species distribution.

BEHAVIOR covers all aspects of the animal's way of life and social structure, from how and where it makes its home, the ways in which it defends its territory, what it eats and how it feeds, to how it raises its offspring, including an illustrated life cycle artwork. The special boxed features in this section include:

• **Prey, predators, neighbors,** or **competitors**—an illustrated list of the animals that the mammal hunts, or those animals that prey on it; or animals that live in the same habitat or that compete for food and habitat.

• **Amazing facts**—learn fascinating facts about the mammal and its way of life.

• **Life cycle box**—all the facts and figures about the mammal from birth to death.

SURVIVAL looks at how and why some animals are under threat and what, if anything, conservationists around the world are doing to help save them. This section also investigates those species that continue to survive against the odds. Where appropriate, there is a map showing the animal's former and current distributions. The survival section also includes special features, such as:

• **At risk**—a chart explaining how the International Union for the Conservation of Nature (IUCN) defines the threat to the animal, such as vulnerable, endangered, or critically endangered.

• **Check these out**—cross-references to related information available in the 20-volume *Exploring Mammals* and the corresponding online database at www.marshallcavendishdigital.com. If the cross-reference is in bold type, the mammal can be found in this book.

CONTENTS

BEAVERS

People are not the only animals that can build structures that change their surroundings. Beavers achieve some amazing feats of engineering with nothing more than nimble paws, a set of built-in chisels, and some natural aptitude.

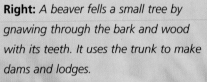

Right: *A beaver fells a small tree by gnawing through the bark and wood with its teeth. It uses the trunk to make dams and lodges.*

Below: *Beavers have thick and oily fur that prevents the skin from getting wet when the beaver is in water.*

Nature's Engineers

KEY FACTS

- **COMMON NAME:** American beaver, Eurasian beaver
- **SCIENTIFIC NAME:** *Castor canadensis, Castor fiber*
- **HABITAT:** Slow-moving rivers, streams, and pools in forested areas.
- **RANGE:** American beaver: Much of North America, small populations have been introduced to parts of Europe and Asia; Eurasian beaver: Small populations are found throughout Europe and northern Asia.
- **APPEARANCE:** Beavers are large rodents. They have a long, flattened, paddle-shaped tail and short, stout legs. Their fur looks shaggy and is very thick, so it can keep the animal warm even in cold water. Large, bright yellow or orange incisors (front teeth) stick out from their mouth. Their small eyes and ears are high on the head.

"In the beginning, Earth was covered with waters in which the muskrat, the otter, and the beaver lived. They dived down into the waters and raised up the mud from which the great spirit Manitou created Earth. The mountains, waterfalls, and caves were the work of the beavers, which were as big as giants." These words are translated from a Native American story about how the world was created. They show that Native Americans were just as amazed with the beaver's engineering skills as people are today. Beavers create lakes, swamps, and lush meadows where there once was only a small stream trickling through dense forests. Few other animals are able to build such large structures and make such changes to their surroundings.

Ancient giants

The idea of giant beavers building the landscape described in the Native American story may sound far-fetched, but some of it is not far from the truth. Animals very similar to modern beavers evolved in the Americas

7

RELATIVES

Beavers belong to a branch of the rodent family tree called the Sciurognathi, which also includes squirrels, mice, and rats. They are more distantly related to other water-loving rodents like capybaras and coypus. The rare mountain beaver is not really a beaver at all. It belongs to a separate rodent family, called the Aplodontidae, and has no close living relatives. Other rodents include:

EASTERN GRAY SQUIRREL (*Sciurus carolinensis*)
A typical tree squirrel, the eastern gray is a nimble animal that lives in the forests across the eastern United States and southern Canada. A similar but slightly larger species lives in western North America.

BLACK RAT (*Rattus rattus*)
Also known as the ship rat, this wily species was originally from India. However, throughout the last thousand years it has spread around the world in close association with people.

HOUSE MOUSE (*Mus musculus*)
House mice originated in Asia but now they live everywhere that people live.

NORTHERN POCKET GOPHER (*Thomomys talpoides*)
Pocket gophers are so called because they have large cheek pouches for carrying food. They live underground in much of central North America and use their teeth to cut through soft dirt.

WOODCHUCK (*Marmota monax*)
Woodchucks, or groundhogs, are burrowing members of the squirrel family. This species is widespread in Canada and the eastern United States and is the largest squirrel in North America.

WATER VOLE (*Arvicola terrestris*)
Water voles are widespread in Europe and Asia. Like beavers, they often live in riverside burrows, but they can also live away from water.

HAZEL DORMOUSE (*Muscardinus avellanarius*)
This small tree-dwelling rodent from Europe spends up to seven months of the year asleep.

about 25 million years ago. They included species like *Castoroides*, which was as big as an American black bear and survived at least until a few hundred thousand years ago. *Castoroides* also had webbed feet and spent much of its time in water. Modern beavers first appeared in Eurasia (Europe and Asia) about seven million years ago. They spread to North America via the land

---

THE TWO SPECIES OF TRUE BEAVERS ARE VERY CLOSELY RELATED— UNTIL RECENTLY SOME SCIENTISTS EVEN THOUGHT THEY MIGHT BE THE SAME SPECIES.

---

bridge that linked the two continents at that time. After the separation of Eurasia and the Americas, the two beaver populations gradually became different enough to count as separate species.

Trapping beavers
While Native Americans respected the beavers, the same cannot be said for European settlers, who saw the animals as a good source of meat and other useful materials. Beaver fur was especially popular for

making coats because it is very warm and waterproof. Beavers also have a pair of glands near their tail that produce a waxy oil called musk. Musk has a strong smell and it was once used as a medicine and for making perfumes.

Close relatives

Beavers are rodents, like rats, mice, squirrels, cavies, and porcupines. The two species of true beavers are very closely related. Until recently some scientists even thought they might be the same species. Biologists thought that the only reason the two forms do not interbreed is because they live on different continents. However, breeding experiments showed that the beavers themselves can tell the difference. They probably use their sense of smell to find members of their own species. People find it less easy to tell the species apart. The only way to be sure is to test their blood.

DID YOU KNOW?

Hairy fish

The Christian Church once stopped its followers from eating meat on Fridays or during Lent, a period of fasting that takes place before the festival of Easter. However, beavers and several other water-dwelling birds and mammals were classified by the priests as fish, and so they were allowed on the menu any time.

Left: *This prehistoric beaver, named* Steneofiber, *lived 25 million years ago.*

Above: *A mountain beaver is not a true beaver. It belongs to a separate rodent family. It lives in a small strip along North America's Pacific coast.*

Left: *A Eurasian beaver. Beavers eat tree bark and young wood. They store small logs underwater and eat them during the winter.*

ANATOMY: American beaver

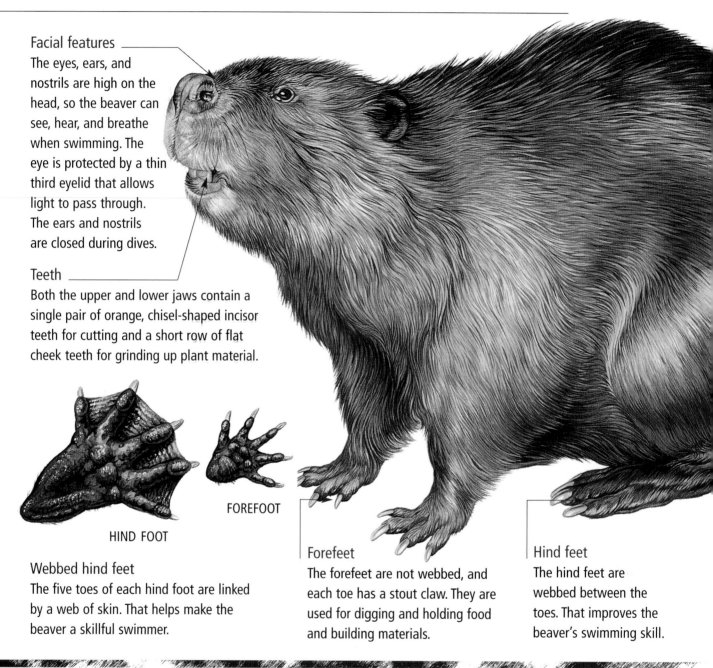

Facial features
The eyes, ears, and nostrils are high on the head, so the beaver can see, hear, and breathe when swimming. The eye is protected by a thin third eyelid that allows light to pass through. The ears and nostrils are closed during dives.

Teeth
Both the upper and lower jaws contain a single pair of orange, chisel-shaped incisor teeth for cutting and a short row of flat cheek teeth for grinding up plant material.

HIND FOOT

FOREFOOT

Webbed hind feet
The five toes of each hind foot are linked by a web of skin. That helps make the beaver a skillful swimmer.

Forefeet
The forefeet are not webbed, and each toe has a stout claw. They are used for digging and holding food and building materials.

Hind feet
The hind feet are webbed between the toes. That improves the beaver's swimming skill.

Skeleton
As with other rodents, the beaver has shoulder and elbow joints that allow freedom of movement. The skeleton is robust but not heavy.

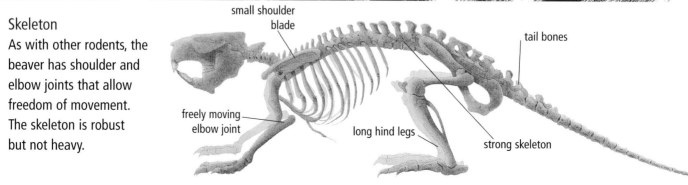

small shoulder blade

tail bones

freely moving elbow joint

long hind legs

strong skeleton

Body

The body is stout and muscular. Beavers are powerful animals for their size. Their muscles are packed with a chemical called myoglobin, which stores oxygen for the animal to use when holding its breath underwater for a long period of time.

Waterproof coat

Beaver fur is incredibly dense—about 77,000 hairs per square inch (about 12,000 per sq cm). There are two layers, a warm under-layer of fine hairs and an outer layer of long, glossy hairs. These two layers create a coat that is not only very warm but also completely waterproof.

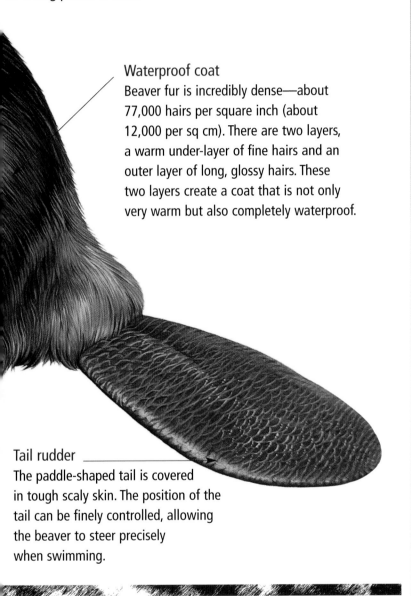

Tail rudder

The paddle-shaped tail is covered in tough scaly skin. The position of the tail can be finely controlled, allowing the beaver to steer precisely when swimming.

Self-sharpening teeth

The incisors grow throughout the beaver's life. They are covered with tough enamel at the front and softer dentine at the back. As the animal gnaws, the teeth wear away faster at the back than the front, creating a razor sharp edge.

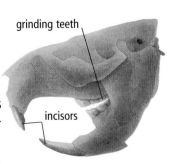

grinding teeth

incisors

FACT FILE

Beavers are the world's second-largest rodents after capybaras. The American beaver (above right) is slightly larger than the Eurasian species. Mountain beavers (above left) are much smaller.

Eurasian beaver

GENUS: *Castor*
SPECIES: *fiber*

SIZE
HEAD–BODY LENGTH: 24–31 inches (61–79 cm)
TAIL LENGTH: 10–18 inches (25–46 cm)
WEIGHT: Average 56 pounds (25 kg)
WEIGHT AT BIRTH: 10–22 ounces (283–624 g)

COLORATION
Rich brown fur that is slightly lighter than the fur of the American beaver.

American beaver

GENUS: *Castor*
SPECIES: *canadensis*

SIZE
HEAD–BODY LENGTH: 31–47 inches (79–119 cm)
TAIL LENGTH: 10–20 inches (25–50 cm)
WEIGHT: 24–66 pounds (11–30 kg)
WEIGHT AT BIRTH: 8–18 ounces (227–510 g)

COLORATION
Rich chocolate brown fur, sometimes with a reddish tinge.

Living beside the water

The two species of true beavers—the Eurasian and American beaver—are natives of the northern hemisphere. They live in similar habitats in Europe, Asia, and North America.

Until a few hundred years ago, there were beavers living in most forested parts of North America, from Canada and Alaska to northern Mexico, and in most of Europe and Russia.

The number of beavers began to decrease as people spread into their range.

> BEAVERS PREFER WOODED AREAS, BUT THEIR MOST IMPORTANT NEED IS WATER.

Trappers killed them for their fur, and their forest habitats were cut down for their timber and to clear the land for farming or buildings. People also killed beavers because their dams damaged fields and ditches and killed useful trees such as conifers. Both species have recovered a little, but they will never be found in the numbers that they once were.

Beavers prefer wooded areas, but their most important need is water. This can be in the form of a river, lake, or marsh. They also live in irrigation and drainage ditches. Beaver dams are now known to have some

Landscape architects

Beavers are one of very few animals capable of making deliberate changes to their surroundings on a large scale. Like people, beavers change the land around them to meet their two most important needs: a safe place to live and breed and a ready supply of food. Both of these requirements are achieved by building dams across rivers or streams to create deep lagoons of still water. The beavers store food in the lagoons and build places to live called lodges. By damming or altering the flow of a stream, beavers cause other changes to their habitat. Areas of previously dry land become flooded with water. That leads to a change in the type of plants that can grow there. Trees such as conifers, which do not like wet conditions, soon die and are replaced by wetland plants such as reeds and rushes, and by different trees, such as willows, alders, and poplars. Over a long time, these new plants dry out the wet ground by drawing out most of water. Then grass begins to grow, forming lush meadows, called beaver meadows.

beneficial effects on the environment, acting as a water purifying system, for example.

Distant relative

Mountain beavers are misnamed. They are not true beavers and do not live in the mountains because they do not like the cold. Mountain beavers dwell in damp wooded valleys where there are plenty of young trees and shrubs.

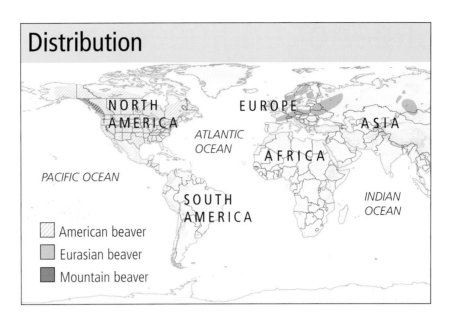

Distribution

NORTH AMERICA

EUROPE

ASIA

ATLANTIC OCEAN

AFRICA

PACIFIC OCEAN

SOUTH AMERICA

INDIAN OCEAN

American beaver

Eurasian beaver

Mountain beaver

Left: *Beavers build lodges out of sticks and mud. The lodges are built beside a lagoon or on an island.*

Below: *Beavers eat the grasses and water plants that grow in the areas flooded by their dams.*

Superior engineers

N ot all beavers build dams. Some areas in which they live have the right conditions already— a deep, still pool, with steep banks in which the beaver can make a safe burrow. However, such readymade homes are few and far between, so beavers build dams, canals, and sometimes islands to create the right conditions.

Lodgings

Where the banks are not high or steep enough to burrow into, the beaver builds a lodge. A lodge is a domed structure of branches and mud, with its foundations below water level. Inside there is a chamber that is well above water level.

The beaver begins building the lodge by pushing sticks and branches into the river bed. The beaver cements them together with mud scooped up in its paws. More and more sticks and mud are added until the lodge eventually rises several feet above the water. The beaver then burrows into the mound and creates a safe living space inside. The walls of the lodge are more than 3 feet (91 cm) thick.

Water surrounding the lodge acts like a moat, detering predators. In winter, the lagoon may freeze and allow predators to walk right up to the lodge, but the mud

lodge

living chamber

2

1

Left: *Beavers use their large front teeth to gnaw through tree trunks, such as those of aspen and willow. New trees grow back quickly.*

Below: *The lodge always has at least one underwater entrance (1) so the beavers can still get into the water even when the surface is frozen over. The lodge may rise as much as 6.5 feet (2 m) above the water (2). Beavers need to add branches from the surrounding woods to keep the dams strong (3). Over a long period of time the dam causes siltation, and meadows begin to develop (4).*

in the walls will be frozen too, making it impossible for even the largest bears to break in.

Dams and canals

A beaver dam is built across a waterway. Like a lodge, a dam is made from branches wedged carefully into the riverbed, then filled out with smaller twigs and mud. The large branches are always angled upstream, making it less likely that they will be washed away by the current. The river current also adds more logs and other debris to the dam.

In addition to lodges and dams, beavers also build canals. These channels are dug in the mud or cleared through beds of water plants. This network of waterways enables beavers to get deep into the surrounding woodland without having to travel over dry land.

beaver meadow

4

3

dam raises level of water

dam

lodge entrance

Timber!

Beavers fell trees to obtain food and building materials. Their technique is so efficient that an adult beaver can bring down a tree with a 6-inch (15 cm) girth in fewer than five minutes. The beaver gnaws around the trunk, making deep grooves and spitting out the wood chips as the typical hourglass form takes shape around the tree. While it works, the beaver supports itself on its hindquarters and broad tail, resting its forelegs against the base of the tree. Beavers can bring down much larger trees but prefer those that grow close to the water's edge. The beaver then strips off the trunk's side branches to make it easier to transport. The beaver uses its network of canals to tow the trunk into place.

mud and stone base

15

Wood eaters

Beavers are strictly plant eaters and eat nearly any part of most plants. When possible, beavers prefer to eat the fresh young shoots of aquatic (water-living) plants, particularly water lilies. Young shoots contain lots of easily digested food, such as sugar and starch. Beavers also eat leaves, twigs, catkins, buds, roots, stems, and bark from plants that grow on land.

Spring and summer are times of plenty, but as the growing season comes to an end and food becomes more difficult

DID YOU KNOW?

Winter storage

Fresh vegetation is hard to find in winter, but wood is one of the few plant materials that is not in short supply. Beavers do not hibernate, and while they can rely to some extent on the fat they build up in the summer, they still need to eat throughout the winter. They spend much of the fall collecting food supplies for a winter larder. Beavers fell a large number of small trees and wedge the logs into mud at the bottom of their lagoon. The cool water softens the wood and also stops it from rotting. The beaver can get to its winter storage using the underwater entrance to its lodge or burrow even when the pool's surface is frozen.

to find, beavers start eating wood. They prefer to eat the wood of trees such as willow, alder, maple, beech, and birch, although they also fell pine trees for food.

Beavers mainly eat cambium. This is the new wood that grows immediately beneath the bark during the summer. Cambium is more nutritious than the older wood deeper inside the trunk. It is soft and contains a lot of sugar, cellulose (the main building material of plant cell walls), and starch. Rather than eat the whole branch, a beaver strips off the newest wood on the outside, leaving a core of older, unwanted wood.

PREDATORS

A stout, meaty body makes beavers attractive prey for large hunters. Despite its big teeth and large claws, the beaver is relatively poor at defending itself from direct attack from predators.

GRAY WOLF (*Canis lupus*)
Wolves hunting alone find beavers traveling out of the water an easy target.

BROWN BEAR, OR GRIZZLY BEAR (*Ursus arctos*)
Brown bears live in much the same kind of areas as beavers and will chase them into the water.

PUMA (*Puma concolor*)
This mighty cat is an excellent hunter and can easily kill a beaver.

GOLDEN EAGLE (*Aquila chrysaetos*)
One of several large birds of prey that may attack young beavers, both on land and in the water.

NORTHERN PIKE (*Esox lucius*)
This large predatory fish is a threat to young beavers as they play in the water close to home.

Left: *Beavers generally feed in water or in a dining area inside their lodges. Out of water, beavers are much more vulnerable to attack from predators.*

Hard to digest

A beaver eats up to 20 percent of its body weight in vegetation a day. Plant material is made up mainly of tough cellulose fibers. Cellulose is hard to digest. Beavers have a long gut, which includes a large sac called a cecum. The cecum contains millions of single-celled microorganisms called bacteria. These microorganisms break down the tough cellulose into sugars, which are easily absorbed by the blood.

Working together

Beaver colonies consist of just one breeding pair and their most recent offspring. Beavers mate for life, and a successful pair can rear more than 100 youngsters in a lifetime. Such success requires a little luck but it also requires teamwork. Families work together to look after the lodge and dam. Even young animals have an instinctive ability to fells trees, but they probably learn the finer points of building by copying their parents. Helping their parents care for younger brothers and sisters also helps yearling beavers develop their own parenting skills. They only get one year to learn, however, because during their second year, when they reach sexual maturity, they are driven away by their parents.

Family life

The family can control up to 0.7 square mile (2 sq km) of territory. Looking after such a large area is hard work, so most territories are smaller, as long as there is plenty of food around.

Female beavers have a reproductive cycle of about two weeks, during which they are ready to mate for just a day. Once pregnant, the female goes on to produce a litter of about three, although there are sometimes more.

BABY BEAVERS: Young beavers, or kits, are born after a 15-week pregnancy. They can swim within hours of birth.

The life of a beaver

COURTSHIP: Courtship begins early in the new year. Any young of previous years that have reached breeding age themselves are driven away to find territories of their own.

Both parents care for the lively young, or kits, which are born with fur and with their eyes open. Kits are nervous to enter the water at first but they soon become expert swimmers. They spend hours playing games that help build up their muscles and improve their swimming and balancing skills. When the youngsters get tired, the mother may allow them to ride on her back or tail. She may even carry them in her forepaws while she walks short distances over land on her hind legs.

ATTENTIVE MOTHER: Close contact between mother and kits helps transfer greasy oils from her fur to theirs, giving their fluffy coats basic waterproofing.

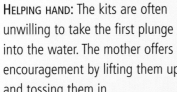

HELPING HAND: The kits are often unwilling to take the first plunge into the water. The mother offers encouragement by lifting them up and tossing them in.

American and Eurasian beavers
MATING SEASON: Spring
GESTATION: 100–110 days
LITTER SIZE: 1–9, but usually 2–4 (a maximum of 6 in European beavers)
WEIGHT AT BIRTH: About 1 pound (454 g)
WEANING: 3 months
SEXUAL MATURITY: 18–24 months
LIFE SPAN: 20 years

Mountain beaver
MATING SEASON: Spring
GESTATION: 28–30 days
LITTER SIZE: 2–4
WEIGHT AT BIRTH: 0.6–0.9 ounce (17–26 g)
WEANING: 6–8 weeks
SEXUAL MATURITY: 2 years
LIFE SPAN: 5–10 years

Trapped for their skins

For thousands of years, people have hunted beavers for meat, for their luxuriously thick, waterproof pelts, and for castoreum (the smelly grease that beavers use to mark their territories, which was used to treat various health problems).

Overhunted

When trapping began it was a small-scale affair. However, in the nineteenth century, the demand for fur coats began to increase as more people in North America and Europe could afford such warm and luxurious garments. Hunters developed new ways to trap beavers, and the numbers killed went up drastically. By 1900 the Eurasian beaver had been almost wiped out. The attack on beavers in the Americas began later than in Europe, but it increased quickly. The value of beaver fur drove pioneering white trappers to push farther into the American wilderness. Settlers followed the trappers, leading historians to believe that the beaver was a crucial factor in the conquest of North America by Europeans.

Above: Beaver furs owned by Canada's Hudson's Bay Company in 1946. The company trapped most of the beavers in North America and was making beaver-fur clothes until 1991.

The famous Hudson's Bay Company traded in beaver fur from Canada. Between 1853 and 1877 it bought and sold three million pelts. By 1904 it was trading almost half a million beaver skins a year.

Environmental effects

By this time, the American species was also on the edge of extinction, and people were beginning to notice side effects. Without the wetlands made by beavers to collect the extra water, flooding became more common. With the beavers gone, the lush meadows that grew around lagoons became overrun by scrubs and forests.

Both the American beaver and the Eurasian beaver are now protected species. In North America, the American beaver has expanded back into much of its former range, but it will never be as common as it once was. In Europe the recovery has been much more

> WITHOUT THE WETLANDS MADE BY BEAVERS TO COLLECT EXTRA WATER, FLOODING BECAME MORE COMMON.

limited because most areas of forest have been built on or turned into farmland. However, Eurasian beavers bred in zoos have been reintroduced to several reserves, and they are doing well.

American beavers are now living wild in Europe. They were deliberately released in Finland, and others escaped from zoos. It is unlikely the two species will interbreed, but conservationists are watching the situation to make sure that American beavers do not push the rare Eurasian beavers out of their habitat.

The mountain beaver has a naturally limited range and has never been a common animal. It causes some damage to forest plantations, but its presence is generally tolerated and its future seems secure.

THEN *AND* NOW

This map shows the current and former distribution of the Eurasian beaver.

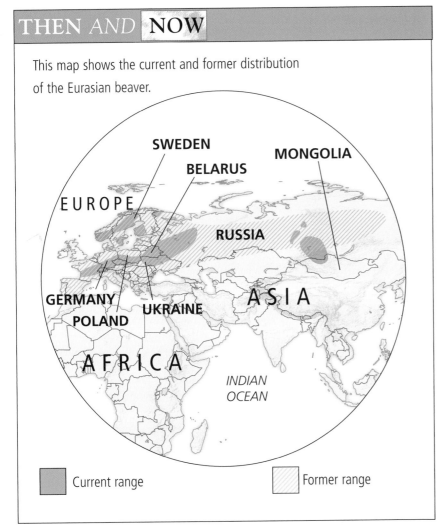

SWEDEN
BELARUS
MONGOLIA
EUROPE
RUSSIA
GERMANY
UKRAINE
POLAND
ASIA
AFRICA
INDIAN OCEAN

Current range Former range

At risk

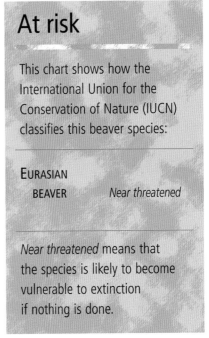

This chart shows how the International Union for the Conservation of Nature (IUCN) classifies this beaver species:

EURASIAN
BEAVER   *Near threatened*

Near threatened means that the species is likely to become vulnerable to extinction if nothing is done.

CHECK THESE OUT

RELATIVES: • Capybaras and coypus • Porcupines • Rats and mice • Squirrels
PREDATORS: • **Brown bears** • **Wolves**

BISON

With two sharp horns backed up by almost a ton of muscle and bone, bison were once very successful animals, but the invention of the rifle changed that forever.

Right: American bison are also often called buffalo. They live in herds. In the past a bison herd might contain many thousands of animals. Now, the herds are much smaller.

Below: A bison's thick skin and woolly fur protect it from cold weather. Native Americans used bison hide to make clothes and shelters.

Hoofed Heavyweights

- **COMMON NAMES:** American bison, European bison
- **SCIENTIFIC NAMES:** *Bison bison*, *Bison bonasus*
- **HABITAT:** American bison: Prairie and open woodland; European bison: Open forest and the edge of woodlands.
- **RANGE:** American bison: Small populations scattered throughout midwestern United States and southern Canada; European bison: Scattered populations in protected areas of Poland, Lithuania, Belarus, Ukraine, Slovakia, and Romania.
- **APPEARANCE:** Very large hoofed animal with massive, low-slung head and curved horns. Deep neck and chest covered in a "beard" of woolly hair. Huge shoulder hump contains the neck muscles that lift the head and large running muscles. Tail has a tuft of long hairs.

F ew wildlife spectacles can rival that of a herd of bison, thousands strong, stretching as far as the eye can see. Such a sight is almost impossible to imagine now, but 200 years ago it would have been common on the prairies of North America. Even a lone bison is an impressive sight. At 6.5 feet (2 m) tall, this powerhouse of an animal has a massive, low-slung head with sharp horns and breath that steams on a cool day.

Bison types

There are two species (types) of bison: the American bison and the European bison, or wisent. The European bison

DID YOU KNOW?

William Frederick Cody (1846–1917), known as Buffalo Bill, was a famous hunter. He specialized in killing American bison for meat to feed workers building the transcontinental railroads. He later used his fame to campaign for the rights of women and Native Americans in the West, and for conservation (protection of plants, animals, and their habitats).

is the taller of the two, with longer legs, but the American bison is generally heavier.

Experts split the American bison population into two subspecies (local forms). The first, called the plains bison, is the bulky beast of "Wild West" legends. Then there is the wood bison—a slimmer, less noticeable animal that lives in southern Canada. It is a forest dweller, with a way of life that is more similar to that of the European bison than its closer American relative.

American bison are often called buffalo, although this is incorrect. The name *buffalo* was used by early explorers who thought the animal looked like the buffalo species living in Africa and Asia. There are several similarities between them. Both bison and buffalo are heavyweight members of the family of wild cattle called the Bovidae.

Ancient ancestors

Fossils are the preserved remains and traces of once-living organisms. Fossils of

Left: A male American bison. Bison have hairy shoulders and heads. The hair keeps the center of the body warm in winter and also makes it look bigger. Males are more hairy than females.

Left: *American bison are now thought of as animals of the prairie, but they were once also common in open woodlands, too.*

ancient bison show that they probably evolved in southern Asia. These first bison evolved from the same hoofed animals that are the ancestors of other types of wild cattle. From Asia the bison spread far and wide. By about one million years ago there were many types of bison living everywhere from Ireland to Korea.

At that time there was a strip of land connecting Asia to North America. At least three species of bison made the crossing and spread through what are now Canada and the United States. One of them was the giant bison, whose horns were 6 feet (183 cm) long. Another, the western bison, was similar to the modern European bison, and this species eventually evolved into the American bison.

RELATIVES

Bison belong to one of the most successful and diverse order of mammals, the Artiodactyla. All members of this order have hooves and an even number of toes. Bison belong to the Bovidae family, which also includes cattle, sheep, and antelope. Other bovids include:

DOMESTIC CATTLE (*Bos taurus*)
Cattle are raised for meat, milk, and leather. They were bred from a wild species called the auroch, which is now extinct.

YAK (*Bos grunniens*)
This stout ox lives in the Himalayas. Thanks to its thick woolly coat, it is able to survive freezing winter conditions that would kill other cattle.

AFRICAN BUFFALO (*Syncerus caffer*)
Considered one of the most dangerous animals in Africa, this buffalo is almost as big as the bison. It lives in herds and is fiercely protective of its young.

KUDU (*Tragelaphus strepsiceros*)
The kudu is one of the largest species of antelope. Males have distinctive corkscrew horns.

EUROPEAN MOUFLON (*Ovis musimon*)
This hardy native Sardinia and Corsica is the ancestor of domestic sheep.

MUSK OX (*Ovibos moschatus*)
A large hairy ox that lives on the freezing tundra. Although it is large like bison and other wild cattle, the musk ox is more closely related to sheep.

COMMON DUIKER (*Sylvicapra grimmia*)
A small hoofed animal that lives a secretive life in the forests of Africa.

ANATOMY: American bison

Horns
Both sexes have sharp, curved horns. The horns have a bony core and an outer covering of keratin (the same tough protein in hair and hooves).

Woolly coat
The hair on the neck and shoulders (above) forms a woolly beard that makes the animal look even bigger than it really is. It comes off in clumps during the spring molt.

Facial features
Female bison have a relatively narrow face, while those of mature bulls (males) fill out and become very wide. The eyes are large but the eyesight is poor. The ears are almost hidden in the hair. The nose has a large area of moist skin called the rhinarium.

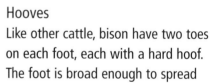

Hooves
Like other cattle, bison have two toes on each foot, each with a hard hoof. The foot is broad enough to spread the animal's great weight and stop it from sinking into soft mud or snow.

AMERICAN BISON

EUROPEAN BISON

The American bison is much stockier than the European bison.

Skeleton
The American bison is extremely front heavy. The tall extensions rising from the backbone between the shoulders provide anchorage for the massive muscles of the shoulder hump. In contrast, the hindquarters are small and narrow.

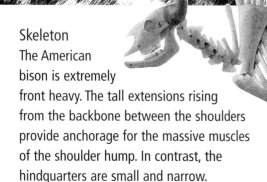

backbone extensions

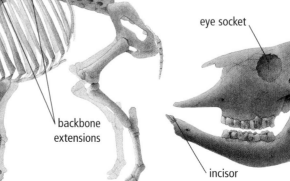

eye socket

incisor

Shoulder hump
The hump is the tallest part of the animal. It contains the enormous muscles needed to support the great weight of the head.

Rump
The American plains bison has a narrow pelvis (hip girdle), making it look even heavier at the front.

FACT FILE

Bison are the largest members of the wild cattle and antelope family, the Bovidae. The American bison (right) is one of the largest American land animals—only polar bears and some brown bears weigh more. European bison (left) are similar in height but they have longer legs and are less bulky.

American bison

GENUS: *Bison*
SPECIES: *bison*
SUBSPECIES: *bison* (PLAINS BISON)
SUBSPECIES: *athabascae* (WOOD BISON)

SIZE
HEAD–BODY LENGTH: 7–11.5 feet (213–350 cm) (males are larger than females)
TAIL LENGTH: 20–30 inches (51–76 cm)
SHOULDER HEIGHT: UP TO 6.5 feet (2 m)
WEIGHT: 1,000–2,200 pounds (450–1,000 kg) (wood bison are lighter than plains bison)
WEIGHT AT BIRTH: 30–70 pounds (14–38 kg)

COLORATION
Very dark brown, sometimes sun-bleached, pale tawny fur on the back and shoulders.

Skull
The huge skull has a large opening at the front that contains the sensitive scent organs connected to the bison's nostrils. The space for the brain is small. There are just two incisor (cutting) teeth in the lower jaw for cropping grass. The two rows of wide molars in each jaw are for grinding grass.

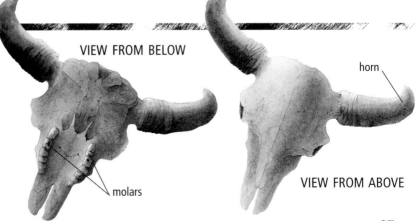

VIEW FROM BELOW

horn

molars

VIEW FROM ABOVE

Home on the range

Bison live on prairies (grasslands) and in open forests, which grow in temperate zones. Temperate zones have a mild, wet climate. Bison are the northern equivalent of the antelope and many other hoofed grazers that live in the hotter, drier African grasslands, or savannas.

Forest life

Modern American bison probably evolved from forest-living animals. Their ancestors looked and lived more like the European bison. The very rare American wood bison subspecies is perhaps most similar to these ancestors. The plains bison have evolved to survive in a different habitat.

Both the European bison and the wood bison prefer to live in forests, where they browse from trees and graze in clearings and in meadows on the forest's edge. The trees shelter the bison from the wind and rain. That helps the wood bison cope with very cold winters.

During the last ice age—a period about 10,000 years ago when much more of the world was covered in ice—forests covered most of central North America. As the ice melted, the trees were replaced with a new habitat—vast swathes of open grassland, or prairie. The bison changed, too.

At risk

This chart shows how the International Union for the Conservation of Nature (IUCN) classifies European bison.

EUROPEAN BISON *Endangered*

Endangered means that this species is likely to become extinct if nothing is done.

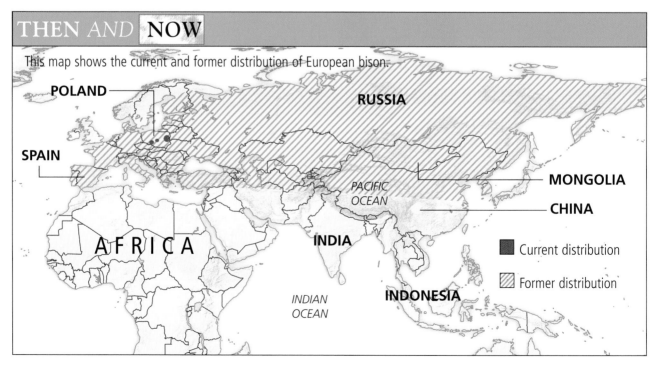

THEN AND NOW

This map shows the current and former distribution of European bison.

POLAND

RUSSIA

SPAIN

MONGOLIA

PACIFIC OCEAN

CHINA

AFRICA

INDIA

Current distribution

Former distribution

INDIAN OCEAN

INDONESIA

Living in the open

Bison already ate grass, but to survive in open country they had to adapt in different ways. They began living in much larger herds, where there was greater safety in numbers. Larger animals also had an advantage. Bigger animals were less likely to be attacked by predators. Males also had to compete more for mates, which often led to fights. The stronger they looked, the more mates they had. So the plains buffalo became slightly heavier and more broad shouldered. The shaggy mane and beard made them look even bigger.

Below: *Most American bison now live in protected areas, such as the National Bison Range in Montana.*

Slaughter and recovery

The American bison population was once huge—probably more than 60 million strong. They were hunted by Native Americans for generations, but it was the arrival of Europeans with guns that spelled disaster for the species. The bison were shot to make way for farmland, and they were shot for sport. Shooting bison in open country required little skill. Instead the contest was about how many a man could kill in a day. In the space of a few decades, the American bison was brought to the brink of extinction.

When there were just a few hundred bison left, Americans realized what they had lost. In 1905 William Hornaday formed the American Bison Society, and began breeding bison in captivity.

In Europe, the range of bison had also shrunk dramatically, and just a few hundred animals survived in two populations in Poland and the Caucasus, a region in southeastern Europe. The first population was destroyed during the battles of World War I (1914–1918), and the second died out in 1927, leaving just 50 or so individuals living in zoos around Europe.

Both American and European bison have been saved by captive breeding. On both sides of the Atlantic Ocean, small populations have been reared in zoos. Then their descendants were released into specially protected lands. The recovery has been widespread in North America, and the wild population now numbers a healthy half million. Europe lacks the large areas of forest habitat needed for a full recovery, but reintroduced populations are doing well in several locations in eastern Europe, particularly in Poland's Bialowieza National Park. The total population remains less than 4,000.

Herd instincts

SHOWING OFF: Before resorting to violence, rival males size each other up. They stand side to side and bellow. Often it is obvious at that stage which animal is bigger and stronger.

Bison are herd animals. The basic social group consists of a few adult females (cows) and their young from recent years. Mature males (bulls) live on the fringes of these groups, only really taking an interest during the breeding season, or rut. A typical herd contains between 20 and 30 bison.

Huge herds

The enormous herds of many thousands of bison that were once seen on the American prairies were the result of many small groups coming together for the sake of safety in numbers. Adult bison have few natural predators, but the young are vulnerable to wolves and mountain lions. In a large herd there is a much better chance of an early warning of an attack.

A TYPICAL HERD
CONTAINS BETWEEN
20 AND 30 BISON.

In day-to-day life, the eldest females are in charge. They decide when the herd moves and when it stops to feed. When the herd is on the move, other adults pay close attention to the youngsters, rounding up stragglers and keeping an eye out for any possible danger.

In huge herds of plains bison, full-blown stampedes tend to happen only in response to unusual conditions, such as attacks from hunters with guns.

Fights break out between bulls to establish which is the most dominant. The bigger and more powerful a bull is, the more chance he has of breeding with as many cows as possible.

HEAD TO HEAD: If neither bull is scared off, a fight breaks out (right). The rivals charge each other, head and horns lowered. They collide with sickening force. Their skulls are thick enough to take such a pounding, but deep stab wounds from the horns can result in one or both bulls dying.

BOWING OUT: The smaller bull (above right) realizes he is outclassed and backs off, with his head lowered in surrender. He lives to fight a more evenly matched challenge another day, while the larger bull wins the right to mate with as many cows as possible.

DID YOU KNOW?

Protective circle

Bison are very protective of their young. When facing a threat, such as a pack of wolves, females gather the youngsters and form a protective circle around them. Their bulky bodies create a living fortress and the bison stand facing outward, their formidable horns ready to fight off the hunters. Adult males join the defense by patrolling the edge of the circle, snorting, pawing the ground, and poised to charge at any predator brave or hungry enough to try to attack.

Plant eaters

PREDATORS

Bison rely on their large size and herd instinct to protect them from most predators. But there are still a few hunting animals that attack young, old, or sick individuals.

GRAY WOLF (*Canis lupus*)
Wolves were once widespread in most of the bison's range. They use teamwork and cunning to slowly wear down the bison's defenses.

GRIZZLY BEAR (*Ursus arctos*)
One of the few carnivorous animals to match the bison in size, the grizzly bear is a subspecies of brown bear.

PUMA (*Puma concolor*)
Pumas, or cougars, hunt alone and risk tackling only very young or sickly bison.

SABER-TOOTHED CAT (*Smilodon*)
This prehistoric hunter would have been a serious threat to young bison. It was about the size of a modern lion but became extinct about 10,000 years ago.

Bison feed during the early morning and at dusk. They prefer to eat mostly grass, but also browse leaves, buds, bark, and tender new twigs from trees and shrubs. Such food is in plentiful supply in spring and summer but can become scarce in winter, when plant growth slows down and the ground is often covered in snow. Bison have to clear patches of grass

by scraping away the snow with their feet or with their head. All this activity makes feeding harder than usual, and bison become very protective of a clear patch of grass.

Eating machine

Grass and leaves are cropped short by the bison's single pair of incisors growing at the front of the lower jaw. There are no front teeth in the upper jaw, just a hard horny plate that acts as a chopping board. Cropped plant material is then chewed and swallowed.

A bison eats as much food as it can in each session. The food collects in the first part of its complex stomach, ready to be processed and digested later on. A herd of bison needs a lot of grass to keep it going, but by moving around a lot, they avoid overgrazing any one patch, and give each area time to regrow before going back.

Below: Bison eat a range of plants, not just grass. They graze with their heads close to the ground, but raise them when they are chewing the cud. That allows them to keep watch for danger.

Chewing the cud

Like many other plant-eating mammals, including most hoofed animals, bison are able to digest tough plant fibers that other animals, such as humans, cannot break down. Their stomach is divided into four chambers. The first chamber, called the rumen, contains bacteria (single-celled organisms). The bacteria are thoroughly mixed with the chewed-up food, which they begin to break down. The bison regurgitates this mixture, the cud, bringing it back from the first stomach chamber to the mouth for more chewing. This process is called chewing the cud. It helps the bacteria work, changing tough plant material into more easily digested sugars.

Late summer rut

Breeding follows a set pattern for bison every year. Courtship and mating occur at times that ensure all the young are born at about the same time. There are several advantages to this. First, the weather is milder during some times of the year—in early spring, young calves are less likely to have to face bad weather. At this time of year there is also a plentiful supply of fresh new grass to help the mothers produce lots of rich, nutritious milk. In addition, being born at the same time as many other young means that each individual calf is less likely to be picked off by a predator.

Mating and birth

Bison mate during an intense period called the rut. For a couple of weeks in late summer, bulls compete for the right to mate with as many cows as possible. Fights are common and the biggest and strongest bulls usually win. They have little time to feed because they must stop other bulls from getting to their mates. By the end the bulls are exhausted.

American and European bison

MATING SEASON: Late summer
GESTATION: 9–10 months (slightly longer in American bison than European)
LITTER SIZE: Usually one, twins are rare
WEIGHT AT BIRTH: 30–65 pounds (14–29 kg)
WEANING: 7–12 months
SEXUAL MATURITY: 2–4 years
LIFE SPAN: 20–30 years

American bison cows are pregnant for about 285 days. European bison have pregnancies that last about 265 days. When it is time to give birth, a female bison leaves the herd for a few days. This period alone allows the mother and calf to bond before mixing with the rest of the herd. The calf is able to walk within a few minutes. By the time it returns to the herd, it can run and recognize its own mother among perhaps hundreds of other females.

The life of a bison

OUTSIDER: Calves are born away from the herd (above left). The mother keeps them away from the other bison for a few days while the two of them learn to recognize each other.

BABYSITTING: Adult bison protect all the calves in the herd. Cows give their milk to the calves of other females, and other adults keep the calves safe from predators.

Cows sometimes suckle calves that are not their own, and other adults work to protect them from predators. The calves form playful gangs in which they acquire some of the skills they will need in adulthood, such as running and fighting. Young females stay with the herd as they grow up, but males begin to move off at about one year old. First, they move to the edges of the herd and then form an all-male bachelor herd that wanders off, only returning when the young males have grown into mature bulls.

CHECK THESE OUT

RELATIVES: • Antelope • Camels and llamas • Cattle • Deer • Gazelles • Goats and sheep • Hippopotamuses
PREDATORS: • **Brown bears** • Pumas • **Wolves**

BROWN BEARS

Below: *Brown bears are huge animals. They are the world's largest land-living hunters.*

KEY FACTS

- **COMMON NAME:** Brown bear
- **SCIENTIFIC NAME:** *Ursus arctos*
- **HABITAT:** Temperate forest, tundra, and mountainous areas
- **RANGE:** Temperate and subarctic zones of the northern hemisphere, from Scandinavia and across northern Asia and North America, extending south along the Rocky Mountains
- **APPEARANCE:** Medium-sized to very large, powerful bear with shaggy brown fur, which may be tipped with gray hair in grizzlies. Face is broad, with narrow tapering snout.

Giant Hunter

The brown bear is among the largest and most feared animals in the world—a creature of awe and legend throughout its enormous range, which covers three continents.

Brown bears once roamed across almost all of Europe and Asia and North America. They feature strongly in the history, culture, and folklore of all these parts of the world.

Different types

Brown bears vary in size and appearance across their huge range. In southern Europe brown bears are relatively small. They rarely weight more than 170 pounds (77 kg) in places such as Italy. Farther north, and east in Siberia, they are much bigger. However the real giants live in North America. The brown bears living along the coast of southern Alaska, such as on Kodiak Island, can be up to 10 times the size of their smaller European cousins, weighing in at around 1,700 pounds (about 770 kg). Kodiak bears grow so large because they have access to a lot of nutritious food, such as the salmon that swim up rivers in huge numbers.

Above: *Brown bears wait beside some rapids. One of their favorite foods is salmon that swim from the sea and head upriver to breed.*

RELATIVES

Brown bears belong to the bear family Ursidae. This is part of the great mammal order Carnivora, which also includes wolves, tigers, seals, and weasels. The other bears are:

POLAR BEAR (*Ursus maritimus*)
One of the largest land-dwelling predators on Earth. Only the brown bears of Alaska's Kodiak Island are bigger. The polar bear is equally at home on solid ground or in frozen seas. It lives in the arctic zone fringing Greenland, North America, Asia, and Norway.

AMERICAN BLACK BEAR (*Ursus americanus*)
These black bears are smaller than brown bears and generally less fierce. They are found in many of the the same places as brown bears but also spread much farther south into the United States.

ASIATIC BLACK BEAR (*Ursus thibetanus*)
The Asiatic black bear is closely related to the American black bear. The main difference between the two species is that the Asiatic bear has a crescent of pale fur on its chest. Thus it is sometimes called the moon bear. Its range overlaps with the brown bear in Asia.

SUN BEAR (*Ursus malayanus*)
A native of Southeast Asia, the sun bear is very shy and spends much of its time in trees. It is named for the round marking on its chest and is the smallest of all bears.

SLOTH BEAR (*Melursus ursinus*)
Sloth bears live in India and surrounding countries. They eat mainly termites and fruit and have a particular preference for honey.

SPECTACLED BEAR (*Tremarctos ornatus*)
This South American cousin of the brown bear is named for the pale markings around its eyes.

GIANT PANDA (*Ailuropoda melanoleuca*)
This shy species has kept scientists guessing about its true classification for years but is now known to belong to the bear family. It lives wild only in the bamboo forests of China.

The differences among brown bears once led people to classify them into more than 100 different subspecies (local forms). Most of these types are no longer recognized, and some, such as the Atlas bear of North Africa and the Mexican grizzly, have become extinct.

GRIZZLIES ARE THE BEST KNOWN SUBSPECIES AND ARE NAMED FOR THE WHITE-TIPPED HAIRS IN THEIR FURRY COAT.

For most Americans, brown bears mean grizzlies. Grizzlies are the best known subspecies and are named for the white-tipped hairs in their furry coat that give them a frosted, or grizzled, appearance.

Relatives
The brown bear's closest cousin is the polar bear, which only became a separate species as little as 100,000 years ago. The two species still have a lot in common, not least that they are both large and ferocious hunters. The American black bear is a more distant relative. While some brown bears can be almost black, they are easily identified by the large hump between their shoulders. This

hump contains mostly muscle and fat. Brown bears nearly always stay on the ground. Young cubs can climb trees but the adults rarely do. They usually walk slowly on all fours but can run very fast for such large animals. Also, they often stand up on their hind legs.

DID YOU KNOW?

Polar bears and brown bears have been able to interbreed in zoos. They have produced hybrids, which are the offspring of different species. Normally, hybrids are infertile (unable to produce fertile young), but polar bears and brown bears are so closely related that their hybrids are able to breed. Biologists think that all bears, apart from giant pandas and spectacled bears, might be able to interbreed in this way.

Left: *Brown bears scratch and rub themselves on tree trunks. The claw marks and hair left behind on the tree are a sign to other bears traveling past that there is already a bear living in the area.*

AMAZING FACTS

• The largest bear ever recorded was a Kodiak bear killed in 1894 that weighed 1,656 pounds (751 kg). Other specimens may be larger, but while bears are alive it is very difficult to weigh them and find out for sure.

Right: *Brown bears are most common in remote mountains and forests where it often gets very cold. The bears have long, thick fur that keeps out the cold and wet.*

ANATOMY: Grizzly bear

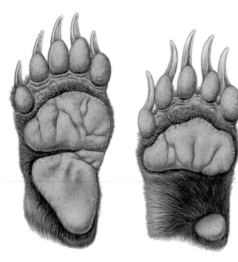

HIND FOOT   FOREFOOT

Heavy body
The bear's body is very bulky and muscular. It is an enormously powerful animal. There is a particularly large hump of muscle at the shoulders.

Paws
All bears have five toes on each foot, and walk with the entire sole flat to the ground, as people do. The pads of the feet and toes are covered in tough skin.

Different sizes
Brown bears living in the cold north tend to be much larger than the bears that live in warmer parts of the world. That helps them endure the cold weather.

Skeleton
The bear's skeleton is built for strength. Its limbs do not have a very wide range of movement but are enormously powerful. The bear can move on two legs or four, and the forelimbs can cross in front of the chest.

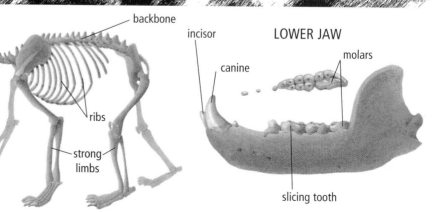

large skull

backbone

ribs

strong limbs

incisor

LOWER JAW

canine

molars

slicing tooth

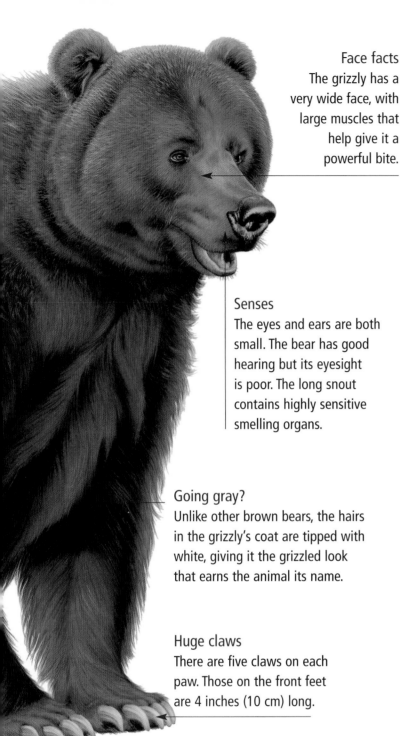

Face facts
The grizzly has a very wide face, with large muscles that help give it a powerful bite.

Senses
The eyes and ears are both small. The bear has good hearing but its eyesight is poor. The long snout contains highly sensitive smelling organs.

Going gray?
Unlike other brown bears, the hairs in the grizzly's coat are tipped with white, giving it the grizzled look that earns the animal its name.

Huge claws
There are five claws on each paw. Those on the front feet are 4 inches (10 cm) long.

FACT FILE

Brown bears vary greatly in size. Grizzly bears can be truly enormous. Standing up on its hind legs, a large male can be 11 feet (335 cm) tall. The Kodiak bear can be even bigger. However, even standing up, Eurasian brown bears rarely exceed 7 feet (213 cm).

Grizzly bear

GENUS: *Ursus*
SPECIES: *arctos*
SUBSPECIES: *horribilis*

SIZE
HEAD–BODY LENGTH: 6–9 feet (183–274 cm)
TAIL LENGTH: 3 inches (7.6 cm)
SHOULDER HEIGHT: 4–5 feet (122–152 cm) on all fours
WEIGHT: 330–860 pounds (150–390 kg)
WEIGHT AT BIRTH: 12–24 ounces (340–680 g)

COLORATION
The fur on the back is a grizzled gray, while underneath the coat is much darker, even black in places. The legs are covered in black hairs. There are three white stripes on the head: one between the eyes and one on each cheek.

Skull and teeth
The skull is long, with plenty of room for the olfactory (smell-sensitive) layer inside the snout and for two rows of grinding molars. The first teeth in each row have sharp edges for slicing meat. At the front of the jaw are eight sharp incisors, or cutting teeth, and four pointed canine teeth. The huge jaw muscles are attached to a ridge on the top of the skull.

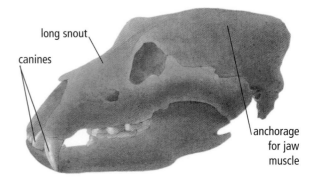

long snout

canines

anchorage for jaw muscle

From forest to tundra

The brown bear is one of the world's most widespread mammals. Until a few hundred years ago brown bears lived throughout most of the temperate regions of North America, Europe, and Asia, where it is neither extremely hot nor extremely cold. In tropical areas, brown bears were replaced by smaller species better able to cope with the heat.

North American bears

Many brown bears live in North America, from Alaska south and east through most of the Canadian states of British Columbia and Alberta and over the border into the United States. Around 30 percent of all the brown bears south of the Canadian border live in the vast expanse of the Greater Yellowstone Ecosystem in Montana and Wyoming. The bears live in dozens of

IN EUROPE PARTICULARLY, THE BEARS HAVE BEEN PUSHED BACK TO JUST A FEW WILDERNESS AREAS, INCLUDING THE ALPS.

Right: *A brown bear and her cub roam the snowy mountain slopes to search for food. Mountain regions are often strongholds for brown bears because there are very few people living there.*

national parks and wildlife reserves in the region and are a big tourist attraction. They also live in pockets of habitat within the Rocky Mountains as far south as Nevada.

In Europe, brown bears still live across an enormous area, but its population is much more dispersed. In Europe particularly, the bears have been pushed back to just a few wilderness areas, including the Alps, Carpathian Mountains, and Abruzzi Mountains. The largest Eurasian population of brown bears lives in Russia.

Diverse habitats

Brown bears are clever at finding ways of doing things and can live in a surprisingly diverse range of habitats. Temperate forests and tundra (treeless frozen plains) offer the best feeding opportunities, but mountains are often preferred because they tend to contain relatively few people.

Too close for comfort

Romania is a stronghold for European brown bears. There are an estimated 7,000 bears in the country—more than in any other country in Europe. Most of these bears live in fairly remote areas, in traditional forest and mountain habitats away from people. In the town of Brasov, however, the local bears have no objection to people at all and live well with extremely close contact. Bears that live in the surrounding forests visit the suburbs almost every night to raid trash cans for food. They may even enter houses. While this shows the species' ability to change to suit their surroundings, it presents a serious problem for both the bears and the people. The bears face threats from road traffic and other hazards, and anyone disturbing a bear unexpectedly might easily be attacked. For example, two men from the town were killed by a female bear infected with rabies.

Distribution

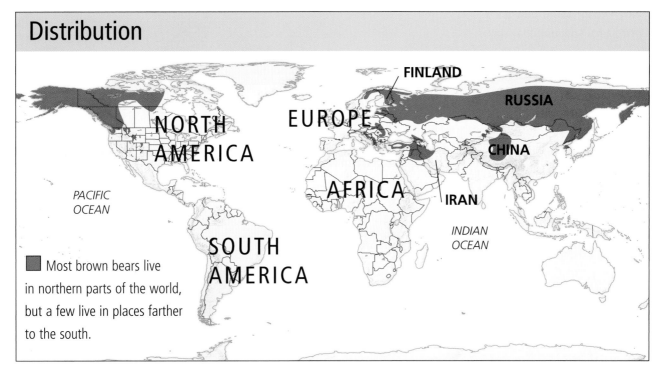

FINLAND

RUSSIA

NORTH AMERICA

EUROPE

CHINA

PACIFIC OCEAN

AFRICA

IRAN

INDIAN OCEAN

SOUTH AMERICA

Most brown bears live in northern parts of the world, but a few live in places farther to the south.

Living alone

Brown bears usually live alone, except for mothers with cubs. Adult bears generally avoid each other so they do not have to share their food supply. However, even lone bears can be sociable from time to time when the conditions are right. Large groups sometimes gather, for example, during the salmon breeding season. At that time food is plentiful, but it is all concentrated around river rapids and waterfalls. As the bears gather at these places, relationships become friendly and even adults play together. However at other times of the year, when food is more scarce and spread over a wide area, bears live in individual home ranges and they can be very aggressive toward strangers who come into their area.

Ranges

The size of a bear's territory depends on the quality of the habitat. In a good habitat, such as Kodiak Island, an adult female can find everything she needs to survive within

The big sleep

Winter is a tough time for bears. Food is in short supply and even if they have fed well during the summer and fall, the bears do not have enough fat to keep them going until spring. If they stay active, they burn a lot of energy and risk dying of starvation. However, if they take it easy, and retire to a cozy den to rest and save their strength, they stand a much better chance of surviving. This long winter rest is a little like hibernation, except that the bears do not go into such a deep sleep as true hibernators. They wake from time to time and sometimes wander outside, hoping for the chance of an easy meal—perhaps an animal that has died of cold or a road-kill victim.

LONE MALES: Adult males always live alone. They regularly pass through the territories of neighboring females. They smell the females' markers to see if they are ready to mate.

FAMILY GROUP: A female bear raises her cubs on her own. She protects them from danger, including adult males.

LEAVING A MARK:
An adult bear marks its territories with urine and droppings. These carry the bear's scent. Bears also rub and scratch tree trunks leaving claw marks and a few hairs behind.

a range of less than 4 square miles (10 sq km). Life is much harder for European brown bears, which live in drier and hotter habitats. They have to range over more than 800 square miles (2,070 sq km). The ranges of neighboring bears tend to overlap. Males have very large ranges that cover the territories of three or four females.

Keeping out of the way

Neighboring bears go to great lengths to avoid each other. They communicate using markers that tell each other they are near, and warn trespassers to stay away. The markers include urine and droppings, which carry the unique scents of individual bears. Bears also scratch and rub tree trunks to leave hair and claw marks.

If these warnings are ignored, then the bears may come to blows. Most fights are between males over mates, but females fight ferociously to defend their cubs, and all bears fight over food. Fighting bears rear up on their hind legs and lunge at each other, wrestling and snarling. They use their teeth and claws to slash at each other and their powerful front legs to grasp one another in a "bear hug."

Hunters and fishers

The ancestors of bears were fierce predators that ate only flesh. Modern bears still have many of the traits of those meat eaters, but they eat a far more varied diet. Scientists describe bears as omnivores, which means they eat all foods. Their choice of food usually depends on what is most easily available at the time.

In summer brown bears eat fruits and fresh leaves. They also eat insects, especially the grubs of bees developing inside hives, and beetle grubs, which bears find by breaking up old

FISHING: The annual salmon run is a period of easy living for American brown bears. The fish are so plentiful that bears travel hundreds of miles to gorge themselves at traditional fishing spots.

ROOTING AROUND: The bear's long claws are perfect for digging up the nutritious roots, bulbs, and tubers of various plants.

logs with their strong claws. In the fall bears eat toadstools and dig up roots, which contain a lot of energy-rich starches. Plant material is difficult for bears to digest because they have a short gut, like other meat eaters. Therefore a lot of the plant food passes directly through the digestive system without being broken down.

Scats

Bear droppings, or scats, often contain recognizable seeds, berries, and leaves. As they

manage to extract only a small amount of nutrient from plant material, bears have to eat a lot to survive.

The alternative is to eat meat, which is easier to digest but can be harder to find. Brown bears are capable of catching swift animals, such as deer, and can bring down

prey as large as moose and young bison. However all this activity takes a great deal of effort, and bears much prefer to save their energy. Nests of small rodents, such as ground squirrels or mice, make a very easy snack, and carrion (already dead animals) provides another supply of meat.

EASY PICKINGS: Carrion (dead animals) makes an easy meal. Bears often feed at roadsides on the remains of animals killed by cars, although they will usually drag the carcasses somewhere quiet to eat.

PREY

Brown bears eat almost anything. A large part of their diet is plant material including fruit, roots, and shoots, but brown bears also hunt for other animals, especially in winter.

ATLANTIC SALMON (*Salmo* species; *Oncorhynchus* species)
Salmon provide a valuable source of protein when they travel upstream to spawn each year. In the shallow water they are easy to catch.

MARMOT (*Marmota* species)
In northern Europe brown bears dig ground squirrels or marmots out of their burrows. In America they target the largest marmot of all, the woodchuck.

ROE DEER (*Capreolus capreolus*)
A regular target for European brown bears, these small deer are common in woodlands throughout Europe.

CARIBOU (*Rangifer tarandus*)
Known in Europe as reindeer, caribou provide a valuable source of meat on the open tundra. Bears usually target the calves.

AMERICAN BLACK BEAR (*Ursus americanus*)
Grizzly bears sometimes kill and eat their smaller cousins.

HONEYBEES (*Apis* species)
Among the bear's smallest prey are bee larvae (young), which are lapped up by the thousand, along with the bees' honey when the bear breaks into a hive.

Fierce competition

Brown bears breed very slowly. It takes a long time to rear a cub and teach it to care for itself, so adult females usually breed only once every three years. As a result, mates are in short supply for males, and competition is fierce.

Having won a female by fighting off his rivals, a male bear mates with the female as many times as he can over the few days she is in estrus (ready to breed). This activity encourages the female bear's ovaries (sex organs) to release eggs. It also provides the male bear with the best opportunity to father a litter of cubs. Other males are never far away, and sometimes the female mates with them, too.

GROWING UP: Cubs spend at least two years with their mother, learning the art of survival. They eventually leave when she is ready to breed again.

Brown bear

MATING SEASON: Summer
GESTATION: 80–226 days, including a period of delayed development.
LITTER SIZE: 1–3
WEIGHT AT BIRTH: 12–24 ounces (340–680 kg)
WEANING: 5–6 months, but will continue taking milk for comfort up to 2 years.
SEXUAL MATURITY: 4–6 years
LIFE SPAN: Up to 35 years in the wild, may live 50 years in captivity.

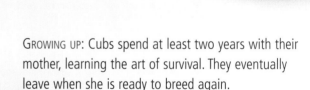

Delayed development

During mating, tiny eggs inside the female bear are fertilized by sperm from the male. However, the eggs do not begin to develop into embryos straight away. Instead there is a delay, which can be anything from a few days to five months. This delay ensures that no matter when the female mated, the young can be born at the best time of year—during late winter while she sleeps in her den. The cubs are then ready to emerge from the den in the warmth of spring, when food is plentiful. Without this delay, the bear cubs would otherwise be born at much less favorable times of the year.

TINY CUBS: Courtship and mating take place in summer, after which the male bear has nothing more to do with his family. Brown bear cubs are extremely tiny. Averaging around 1 pound (451 g), they are no bigger than a rat—as little as 0.25 percent the weight of their mother. They are born while she sleeps and instinctively crawl to her teats. The mother can cuddle and suckle her babies for several weeks without ever properly waking up.

The life of a brown bear

FUN AND GAMES: By the time they come out of the den in late spring, the cubs are full of fun, but they never stray far from their mother.

Giant killing

Brown bears now occupy a fraction of the huge range they had in the past. Throughout Europe, Asia, and North America they have been forced out of areas where people have settled, and their populations have been broken up. Bears have been hunted for thousand of years, mostly out of fear, but also for their skins and fur. People also shoot bears for sport. Hunting continues in many parts of the brown bear's range. Sometimes hunting is carried out with legal permission, but more often it is done illegally. Farmers often want to shoot bears instead of preserving them because the bears threaten their livestock.

In danger

Brown bears have been wiped out completely in Mexico and now the most threatened brown bear population lives in the Pyrenees mountains between France and Spain. In 1997 and in 2005, bears from Slovakia were released in the area to boost the population, despite opposition from local

Right: Bears are not fussy eaters. They often rummage through garbage to find scraps of food. This brings them close to towns where they are sometimes shot by frightened residents.

PAPER, WOOD, AND PLASTIC
NO FOOD WASTE

AMAZING FACTS

- Grizzly bears may look heavy and lumbering, although they can run as fast as a horse, but only over a short distance.
- Only young brown bears can climb trees. The adults are too heavy to lift themselves up.
- Brown bears of Alaska's Kodiak Island are the largest in the world—they beat polar bears to the title of biggest predatory land animal.

THEN AND NOW

This map shows the current and former distribution of the brown bear in the United States.

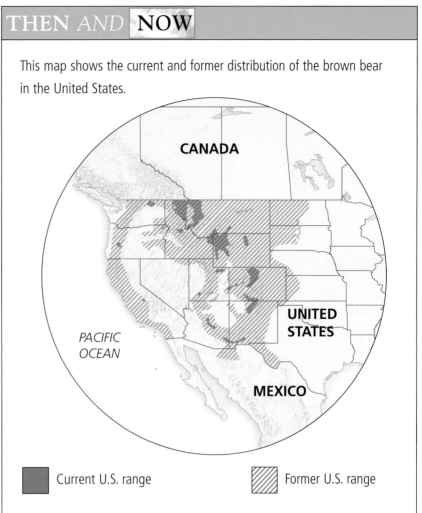

☐ Current U.S. range   ▨ Former U.S. range

farmers. The whole Pyrenean population probably numbers no more then 20 animals.

Killer bears

Bears and people tend not to mix well. At least a few people are killed by bears every year. Grizzly bears are considered some of the most dangerous animals in North America. However, many more people die as a result of insect bites or diseases caused by rats. Bears do not normally hunt humans to eat, but they attack people that get in their way or too close to their young.

There is little anyone can do to save themselves from a grizzly. Some people recommend climbing a tree or making a lot of noise, while others suggest backing away as quietly as possible. Even most guns are no defense.

CHECK THESE OUT

RELATIVES: • American black bears
• Bears, small • **Pandas** • **Polar bears**
PREY: • Deer • Goats and sheep

DOLPHINS

Dolphins are very social mammals that form strong bonds and live in groups called pods. Using sound and touch, dolphins communicate constantly with other members of their pod. If a dolphin is injured or threatened, other pod members rush to its defense.

Below: *Dolphins leap out of the water to take a breath through the blowhole on top of their head.*

KEY FACTS

- **COMMON NAME:**
Dolphin
- **SCIENTIFIC NAME:**
Family Delphinidae
SPECIES: There are about
35 species.
- **HABITAT:** Oceans,
coastal waters,
and rivers
- **RANGE:** All oceans
except near the poles,
and major rivers in Asia
and South America.
- **APPEARANCE:** Dolphins
have a streamlined body
for cutting through
water. Their forelimbs
are flippers and they do
not have hind legs. The
tail has two fleshy fins
called flukes. Unlike
most larger whales,
dolphins and porpoises
have teeth.

Underwater Mammals

Some people think that dolphins are fish, probably because they have fins and live underwater. However, dolphins are mammals. Over the course of evolution, their body form has come to resemble that of fish. This form is best for moving through water. Instead of legs, dolphins have flippers and a wide tail for swimming. Unlike fish, which use gills to obtain oxygen from water, dolphins breathe air like other mammals. Every so often, dolphins come to the surface to breathe, taking in air through a large nostril, called a blowhole, on the top of their head. When diving, the blowhole is kept closed by a muscular flap.

Dolphins are members of the whale order, Cetacea. Ceteceans are divided into two main groups, toothed whales (Odontoceti) and baleen whales (Mysticeti). Dolphins and a few small types of whales are toothed whales. Other toothed whales include orcas (or killer whales), sperm whales, and belugas.

Baleen whales do not have teeth. Instead they have long plates of baleen, which are fringed curtains of tough protein called whalebone that hang inside the mouth. Rather than biting and chewing their food, baleen whales use these plates to filter small food items from the water, such as tiny shrimplike animals called krill.

Above: *In some species of dolphins, an individual will investigate unknown objects, such as a photographer, and then report back to the pod.*

RELATIVES

Dolphins belong to an order of mammals called Cetecea (whales). There are two main types of ceteceans: toothed whales, such as dolphins, and baleen whales, which do not have teeth. Nondolphin ceteceans include:

GRAY WHALE (*Eschrichtius robustus*)
This animal is a baleen whale. Instead of teeth, it has long fringed plates hanging from the upper jaw. These plates sieve food from seawater.

ORCA, OR KILLER WHALE (*Orcinus orca*)
Many scientists think that orcas are the largest dolphins. Others group orcas and the closely related pilot whales separately. All, like dolphins, are toothed whales.

RIGHT WHALE (family Balaenidae)
Another type of baleen whale, the right whale has a huge head. Right whales and the related bowhead whales have the largest mouths in the animal kingdom.

RORQUAL (*Balaenoptera* species)
Rorquals are huge baleen whales. One type is the blue whale, the largest animal that has ever lived.

SPERM WHALE (*Physeter catodon*)
This huge toothed whale is the world's largest hunter.

Different dolphins

Dolphins and porpoises are divided into four groups: oceanic dolphins, coastal dolphins, river dolphins, and porpoises. These families contain dolphins that look the same but live in different ways. However, it is likely that the members of some of the groups are not all closely related. For example, biologists believe that the different types of river dolphins probably evolved separately from different groups of coastal and oceanic dolphins. Most river dolphins have small dorsal fins—the fleshy blade that sticks out from the back—and very long snouts filled with lots of small teeth. However, they probably look the same just because they live in the same types of habitats. Biologists think that river dolphins resemble early toothed whales.

The largest dolphins

The largest dolphins belong to the oceanic dolphin family, including bottlenosed dolphins and spinner dolphins. Many biologists think that coastal dolphins, such as the

---

COASTAL DOLPHINS USE SIGHT TO FIND FOOD, BUT OCEANIC DOLPHINS FIND FOOD USING ECHOLOCATION.

---

humpbacked dolphin, are a subgroup of oceanic dolphins. The main difference between the two groups is that coastal dolphins rely on sight to find food, while oceanic dolphins use an echolocation system, or sonar.

Orcas and other larger toothed whales, such as pilot whales, are also sometimes included with the oceanic dolphins. However, these whales have fewer teeth than most dolphins, so they are often grouped

as a completely separate family, Globicephalidae.

Porpoises are generally smaller than dolphins. The main differences between the two groups are that porpoises have round heads and they do not have the pointed, beaklike snouts of dolphins. Most dolphins also have twice as many teeth as porpoises.

Below: *Dolphins may leap out of the water and land on their back or sides. This behavior is called breaching and is also a common behavior in whales.*

DID YOU KNOW?

Ancestors

Dolphins and other whales evolved from land mammals about 60 million years ago. Some of these land mammals began living along the coast and spending time in shallow waters. Eventually some evolved to live completely in water, and their bodies changed in such a way that they could not survive on land. The closest living relatives of whales are hippopotamuses, which are placed in the order Artiodactyla (even-toed ungulates). Whales are therefore highly evolved artiodactyls.

The oldest-known cetecean was an animal called *Pakicetus*, which lived about 50 million years ago. Although all cetaceans are thought to have evolved from such creatures, *Pakicetus* looked more like an otter, with short, wide legs used for paddling. Unlike present-day cetaceans, *Pakicetus* probably came out of the water onto land.

ANATOMY: Common dolphin

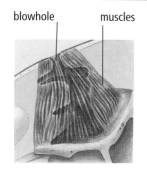

blowhole   muscles

Blowhole
The blowhole (left), a crescent-shaped nostril on top of the dolphin's head, is connected to the dolphin's mouth. It is lined with muscles that seal the blowhole when the animal dives underwater.

Fin
The fin is made of cartilage and firm fat. It helps the dolphin stay upright when swimming through the water quickly.

Melon
Inside the dolphin's head is a lump of oil and fat called the melon. It focuses the sounds the dolphin makes to search for food and to stun prey.

Eyes
The dolphin's eyes can move independently of each other and can look straight ahead.

Ears
A small (invisible) opening connects the ears to the outside. Sound does not reach the ears through this hole. Instead, sound travels to the ears through the jawbone.

Flippers
The flippers are used for steering and contain five "finger" bones. The bones of the back legs have been lost completely during evolution. In some individuals, tiny pieces of the pelvic girdle remain as evidence of hind legs.

Head
Dolphins have a large head compared with the rest of the body.

Skeleton
Many of the bones at the top of the dolphin's spine are fused so the head and neck area are held solidly as the dolphin powers through the water.

Skin

Blood vessels project into the blubber, carrying away or bringing heat to the fatty zone as needed.

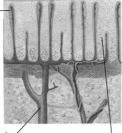

blood vessel   blubber

The skin has a thick layer of fat, called blubber, which keeps the body warm in cold water.

Streamlined body

The dolphin's torpedo-shaped body lets the animal move through the water smoothly.

Flukes

The tail has two lobes, called flukes, sticking out sideways. The dolphin powers itself along by moving the flukes up and down. They are made from tough fibers.

BOUTU

HARBOR PORPOISE

COMMON DOLPHIN

Skull

The skulls of dolphins and porpoises are asymmetrical, with the blowhole located at the top and slightly to the left. The harbor porpoise has far fewer teeth than the common dolphin, which has around 200.

Teeth

Many dolphins have sharp, pointed teeth (top). Porpoise teeth (below), however, are flattened into a spade or chisel shape at the tips.

Roaming river and sea

Dolphins and other whales spend their whole lives in water. Unlike seals, walruses, and other aquatic mammals, which also live in water, dolphins cannot live for long outside of water. If they become stranded on land, the weight of their bones, muscles, and fat may crush internal organs and squeeze the air out of the lungs, and they die.

Below: *The Atlantic spotted dolphin lives in the Atlantic Ocean in tropical to warm temperate waters.*

Ocean travelers

Dolphins and porpoises inhabit every ocean except the coldest waters of the Arctic and Antarctic. Although these cold waters often contain huge amounts of food at some times of the year, dolphins prefer to eat in warmer waters, where there is a good supply of food throughout the year.

Many large whales, primarily giant baleen whales, migrate (travel) between the cold and warm feeding grounds every year. Many oceanic dolphins also travel over huge distances each year. However, these journeys are not the same as migrations. A migration is a round trip that an animal takes to find food, mates, or other resources. At the end of each trip, the animal always returns to where it started. Generally, dolphins do not travel in this way—they just move around a lot. Many species, such as bottlenosed dolphins, do not live in one area. Instead, they roam over huge distances and are found in all the warm and temperate waters of the world.

Distribution

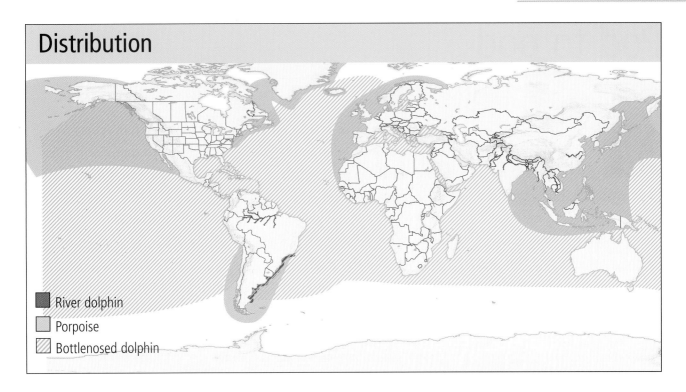

- ■ River dolphin
- ▢ Porpoise
- ▨ Bottlenosed dolphin

Coastal dolphins, such as humpbacked dolphins, eat fish and other animals that live in shallow water. They stay close to the shore and generally inhabit much smaller ranges.

Inland waterways

Living in freshwater is very different to living in sea water, which is full of salt. Most dolphins can survive for only short periods in freshwater. However, a few coastal dolphins swim into the mouths of large rivers, where the tide mixes with freshwater. For example, the Atlantic humpbacked dolphin swims into the Congo River and other rivers in western Africa. The tucuxi, a coastal dolphin,

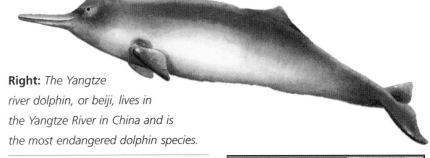

Right: *The Yangtze river dolphin, or beiji, lives in the Yangtze River in China and is the most endangered dolphin species.*

is also often present in the Orinoco and Amazon rivers.

Most river dolphins live far from the ocean and never taste salt water. The Amazon river dolphin lives in the Amazon and Orinoco rivers and is often seen hundreds of miles upriver in the foothills of the Andes. In Asia, the waters of the Ganges and Indus rivers, which form in the Himalayan mountains, are home to two species of river dolphins.

AMAZING FACTS

- Dark-skinned dolphins live in deep water, while those with dark and pale patterns live in the sunny water at the surface.
- Indopacific humpbacked dolphins come out of the water to slither over mud banks that get in their way.
- Ganges and Indus river dolphins live in muddy water and are almost blind.

Pod to pod

Most dolphins and porpoises live in large groups called pods. Only river dolphins regularly spend long periods on their own. Most pods have about 20 dolphins, but some contain as many as 100. Sometimes, many pods gather to form huge crowds of more than 1,000 dolphins. Different species of dolphins sometimes swim together, but there is usually little social interaction among species.

Pod structure

Mothers with small calves swim at the center of the pod so they are protected from predators, such as sharks and killer whales. Older and larger males swim on the outside. Younger males, however, generally leave the pod and form separate pods. Young females from the main group often join this second pod, but most rejoin their mothers' pod when they become fully grown adults. Males may join other pods that pass or they might also rejoin the pod they were born into.

Scientists do not fully understand how dolphin society is organized. Adult males often leave their pods for a short while to mate with females in another pod.

The social system seems to be flexible, with many dolphins moving from pod to pod.

Keeping in touch

Dolphins work together to hunt fish. When swimming fast, they leap out of the water to take breaths. Members of the pod often leap at more or less the same time, so they all land back in the water together. That makes sure the dolphins are always all ready to begin an attack if they spot a school of fish.

Dolphins communicate using a language of groans, whistles, and clicks. These noises are mainly ultrasound, which is too

DID YOU KNOW?

Helping friends

Dolphins are intelligent mammals and sometimes appear very friendly toward people who are lucky enough to swim with them. There are also many stories about dolphins helping drowning sailors swim back to the surface, which may be true because dolphins often help injured family members to the surface. The helper dolphins move beneath the injured one and push it up. They also help it swim if it is too weak to do so alone.

high-pitched for people to hear. Studies of captive dolphins have shown that loud noises accompanied by jaw clapping and tail slapping mean that the animals are angry. Dolphins also make loud twitters when they are excited and emit soft chirping sounds when they greet other dolphins.

Each dolphin produces a unique whistle that identifies it to the other members of the pod. When a dolphin is in trouble, such as under attack by a shark or killer whale, the other members of the pod rush to help the victim.

WORKING TOGETHER: Bottlenose dolphins work together to round up their fish prey. The dolphins swim around the school of fish in tighter and tighter circles. That forces the fish into a smaller area. The dolphins then move in and catch the fish with their teeth.

Sonic hunters

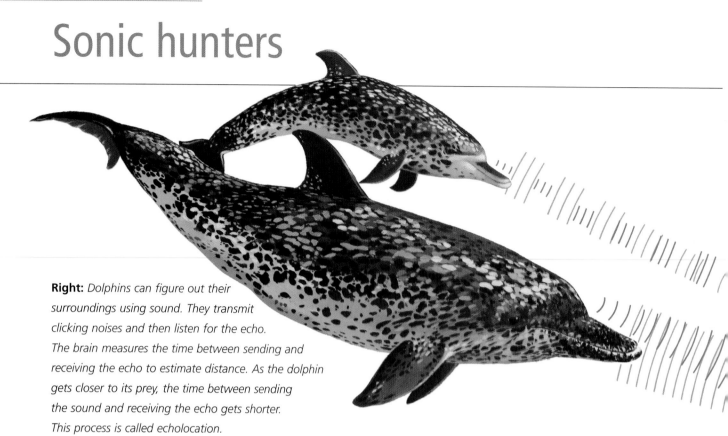

Right: *Dolphins can figure out their surroundings using sound. They transmit clicking noises and then listen for the echo. The brain measures the time between sending and receiving the echo to estimate distance. As the dolphin gets closer to its prey, the time between sending the sound and receiving the echo gets shorter. This process is called echolocation.*

PREY

Dolphins are hunters. Most of them eat a diet of fish, but some also eat other small swimming creatures.

MACKEREL (family Scombridae)
These fast-swimming fish gather in huge schools near the surface of the ocean.

ANCHOVIES (family Engraulidae)
These small relatives of the herring swim in large schools in shallow water not far from the coast.

FLYING FISH (family Exocoetidae)
These fish swim close to the surface. They are named for their ability to glide through the air on their fins. When a predator, such as a dolphin, comes near, the fish leap out of the water to escape.

OCTOPUS (class Cephalopoda)
While most dolphins are fish eaters, a few coastal species eat octopus and crustaceans, such as lobsters, that live in shallow water.

Most dolphins are fish eaters. They use echolocation, a form of sonar in which reflected sound is used to detect prey, such as schools of fish. Members of the pod often work together to round up their prey. They swim around the fish in smaller and smaller circles to pack them into a tight school. Then the dolphins take turns swimming through the school, snapping up fish. They may stun the fish with a powerful sound wave to make catching them easier.

A dolphin's long snout is filled with small, sharp teeth,

which are used only for snatching up small fish. The prey is then swallowed whole. Porpoises are also fish eaters. Their teeth are chisel-like blades, which act like shears. They are better for catching and holding their prey of larger, smoother fish.

The sound waves emitted by the dolphin pass through the soft parts of a fish but reflect off the hard parts, such as the bones.

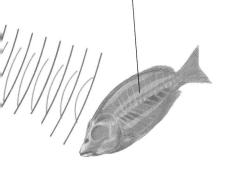

Squid eater

Risso's dolphin is one of the few oceanic dolphins that does not eat fish. These dolphins hunt for squid. They have no teeth on their upper jaw and only a few on the lower one. Instead of biting, these dolphins suck squid into their smooth mouth.

Coastal dolphins have fewer teeth than oceanic ones. Their teeth are also rougher, which helps them grab and hold bottom-living prey, such as crabs and octopuses.

DID YOU KNOW?

Sonar system

All dolphins use a sonar system called echolocation to find food and large objects in dark or muddy water. Oceanic dolphins have the most sensitive sonar system. Coastal dolphins, which live in bright, shallow water, use their eyes to spot food. Some river dolphins are nearly blind, and they rely almost entirely on sonar to find food in murky river water.

Sonar is a system that uses reflected sound to obtain information about the surroundings, similar to the system used in submarines. The dolphin makes clicking noises using a sac beneath the blowhole. These noises pass through the melon in front of the sac. The melon acts like a lens and focuses the sounds into a beam. This beam echoes off objects in front of the dolphin. The echoes are waves in the water, and when these waves come back to the dolphin, they make the animal's jawbone vibrate. These vibrations are picked up by the ear. The time it takes for echoes to return indicates to the dolphin how far away an object is. The loudness of the echo also tells the dolphin how big the object is. Large masses, such as a school of fish, produce louder echoes. Echolocation can also be used to tell the direction of movement of prey.

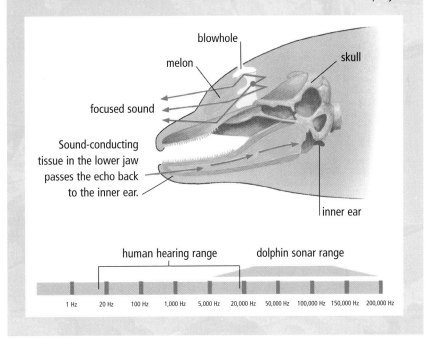

River dolphins also feed on a variety of different foods, including flatfish and turtles. The Amazon river dolphin is the only species of dolphin to have different types of teeth. Their front teeth are sharp and their back teeth are flat.

Birth helpers

Most dolphin species have a breeding season. Some mate in spring and fall, while others mate in summer. During the breeding season, males become more aggressive with each other and smack their jaws loudly if a rival gets too near. Males and females each mate with several dolphins, and mating takes place belly to belly. Most species of dolphins have pregnancies that last for almost a year, and females breed once every two or three years.

Midwife

About halfway through the pregnancy, a female dolphin chooses another adult female in the pod to help as a midwife. All midwives have had a calf themselves and are often related to the pregnant dolphin. The two females move to the edge of the pod and spend most of their time together for the rest of the pregnancy.

Birth

A few weeks before the calf is due, the mother flexes and stretches her body, which helps make sure that the baby is in the right position for birth. The calf is born tail first, so its blowhole stays out of the water for as long as possible. Birth takes about two hours. The calf's eyes are open at birth, and once it has taken its first breath with the help of its mother, it can swim.

The calf's body is covered with a stubble of tiny hairs, which soon falls off. The calf is suckled by its mother for up to 18 months. At four months it begins to eat solid food. The growing calf swims under its mother, where it is pulled along by the water currents that the mother makes as she swims.

The life of a dolphin

HELP AT BIRTH: During labor (below), the mother is helped by a midwife, another female dolphin. After birth, the mother bites through the umbilical cord and begins to push the calf to the surface.

OPENING TIME: Once on the surface, the calf's blowhole opens so it can breathe. The calf is soon able to swim on its own.

HEAVY CALF: Without any air in its lungs, the newborn calf is heavier than the water and would sink if its mother did not push it up to the surface to take its first breath.

DID YOU KNOW?

Squirt, not suck

Because of the shape of a baby dolphin's long snout, it cannot suck on its mother's teat. Therefore, dolphin mothers pump milk into the mouths of their young. The teats are hidden inside slits under the mother's tail. The calf rolls its tongue around the teat, making a channel for the milk to run along, and muscles in the mother's teat squirt milk into the channel. At first the calf feeds every 20 minutes. Dolphin milk is very fatty compared with human breast milk. The rich milk enables the calf to double its weight in the first two months of its life.

Common dolphin
BREEDING SEASON: Mates in spring and fall
GESTATION: 10–12 months
LITTER SIZE: 1
EYES OPEN: At birth
FIRST SOLID FOOD: 6 months
SEXUAL MATURITY: 12 years
LIFE SPAN: 50 years

Franciscana
BREEDING SEASON: Mates in summer
GESTATION: 9 months
LITTER SIZE: 1
EYES OPEN: At birth
FIRST SOLID FOOD: 8 months
SEXUAL MATURITY: 3 years
LIFE SPAN: 16 years

Fishing threat

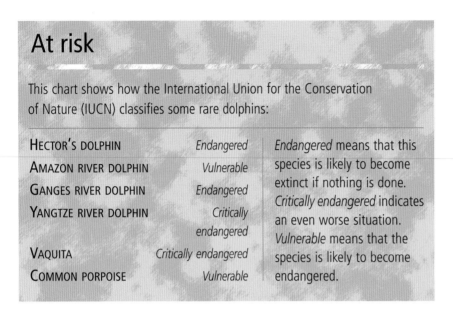

At risk

This chart shows how the International Union for the Conservation of Nature (IUCN) classifies some rare dolphins:

HECTOR'S DOLPHIN	*Endangered*
AMAZON RIVER DOLPHIN	*Vulnerable*
GANGES RIVER DOLPHIN	*Endangered*
YANGTZE RIVER DOLPHIN	*Critically endangered*
VAQUITA	*Critically endangered*
COMMON PORPOISE	*Vulnerable*

Endangered means that this species is likely to become extinct if nothing is done. *Critically endangered* indicates an even worse situation. *Vulnerable* means that the species is likely to become endangered.

THEN AND NOW

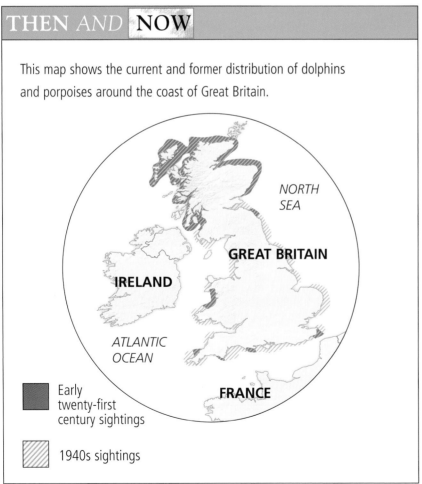

This map shows the current and former distribution of dolphins and porpoises around the coast of Great Britain.

NORTH SEA

GREAT BRITAIN

IRELAND

ATLANTIC OCEAN

FRANCE

Early twenty-first century sightings

1940s sightings

Many dolphins and porpoises are threatened with extinction. Pollution has reduced the numbers of river dolphins, and all species are now under threat. Pollution and other human activities have also reduced the population of coastal dolphins, especially along the coasts of developed countries. For example, dolphins are frightened away from rich coastal feeding grounds by leisure boats. In shallow water, the engines cause a lot of underwater noise that confuses the dolphins. They sometimes investigate the sounds and are killed by the propellers.

Drowned at sea

Fishing is by far the biggest cause of dolphin deaths. Each year, hundreds of thousands of dolphins are killed accidentally by commercial fishers because dolphins get trapped inside fishing nets and drown.

One of the worst problems is caused by gill nets, which may be thousands of feet long and trap anything in their path. The vaquita, also called

Dolphin friendly

New dolphin-friendly fishing techniques have been developed to reduce the number of dolphins and porpoises accidently killed by tuna fishers. In many parts of the world, fishing boats look for schools of dolphins because they know that shoals of tuna are often swimming underneath them. Both tuna and dolphins are caught in huge net bags, called purse seine nets. The mesh of the net is too large for the dolphins to see or detect by sonar. However, new nets are being used with a panel of fine mesh called a Medina panel. The dolphins can see this panel and they jump over the net before they get caught. The fishing technique used is as follows:

(**1**) Tuna (with the dolphins) are spotted by a helicopter and the fishing boat sends out inflatable boats to round up the fish.

(**2**) An inflatable boat draws a purse seine fishing net around the fish and the dolphins. The other inflatables block the escape of the tuna and dolphins.

(**3**) As the net is pulled in, the dolphins gather near the visible Medina panel, ready to leap to safety over the rim of the net.

(**4**) Most of the dolphins can now jump clear of the net. Some are given a helping hand from divers. Many calves still get caught in the net, however, because they are too small to jump with their mothers.

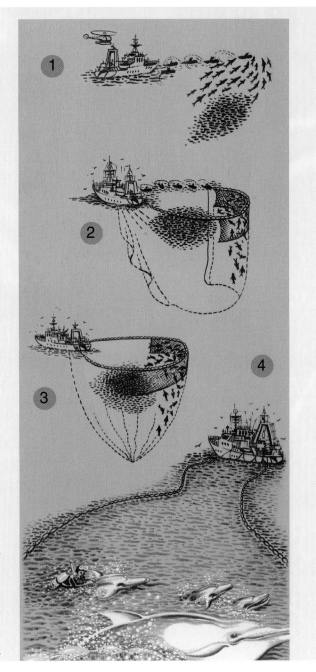

the cochito or Gulf of California porpoise, is one of the rarest of ceteceans and has been nearly wiped out by gill netting in the Gulf of California. In recent times, the nets have been made shorter and fitted with pingers, which produce a high-pitched sound that scares away dolphins and whales.

Another big dolphin killer is tuna fishing. In the Pacific Ocean, yellowfin tuna often swim beneath pods of spinner dolphins. The tuna and dolphins are then herded into a huge net bag. In the past, 100,000 dolphins were killed in this way every year. Dolphin-friendly fishing techniques have reduced the number killed, but many dolphins still die in nets.

CHECK THESE OUT

RELATIVES: • Gray whales • **Killer whales** • Right whales • Rorquals • Sperm whales

FRUIT BATS

Flying Fruit Eaters

Fruit bats can be distinguished from other bats by their fruit diet and by their foxlike faces. These bats rely on excellent eyesight and a keen sense of smell to find their fruity food.

Fruit bats feed on plant foods, unlike most bats, which hunt insects. Fruit bats are also the largest bats and most are sociable, gathering in large groups.

In parts of the tropics, an amazing sight may be seen at sunset. Trees in which fruit bats are resting come alive as the bats fly off together on their nightly search for fruit. However, not all fruit bats behave in this way. With more than 170 species, fruit bats are a large and varied group, but all are vegetarians, feeding on fruit, flower nectar, and pollen. Fruit bats live only in tropical and subtropical Africa, Asia, and Australia.

Above: *This spectacled flying fox is enjoying a juicy fruit. Fruit seeds pass through the bat's gut and when excreted may land far from the tree that bore the fruit. The spectacled flying fox spreads the seeds of at least 26 Australian species of rain forest trees in this way.*

KEY FACTS

- **COMMON NAME:** Egyptian fruit bat (also known as Egyptian rousette bat)
- **SCIENTIFIC NAME:** *Rousettus aegyptiacus*
- **SPECIES:** More than 170 species of fruit-eating bats, including flying foxes, hammer-headed bats, tube-nosed fruit bats, and epauletted bats; the smaller group of long-tongued bats includes blossom bats
- **HABITAT:** Forests, caves, scrublands, and urban areas
- **RANGE:** Africa and western Asia
- **APPEARANCE:** Small bat about 6 inches (15 cm) long, with thick fur; doglike face with large eyes and ears; dark brown to gray fur on back, with paler fur on underparts; males have a collar of buff or yellowish fur around the neck.

RELATIVES

Fruit bats (family Pteropodidae) make up the suborder of megabats. The larger group of microbats, containing around four-fifths of all bats, includes:

VAMPIRE BAT (*Desmodus rotundus*)
Living in Central and South America, vampire bats lick the blood of birds and mammals. They bite victims and have a substance called an anticoagulant in their saliva (spit) that stops blood from clotting.

COMMON PIPISTRELLE (*Pipistrellus pipistrellus*)
The most common bat in Europe, this little bat roosts in attics and barns.

SPECTRAL BAT (*Vampyrum spectrum*)
Once thought to be a bloodsucker, this false vampire bat hunts rodents, birds, and other bats.

HOG-NOSED BAT (*Craseonycteris thonglongyai*)
The hog-nosed bat of Thailand is the world's smallest bat, weighing just 0.07 ounce (2 g).

GREATER HORSESHOE BAT (*Rhinolophus ferrumequinum*)
Living in Europe, Asia and North Africa, these bats migrate long distances to hibernate.

TENT-MAKING BAT (*Uroderma bilobatum*)
Living in Central and South America, these bats roost in "tents" made by biting through palm or banana leaves so that they droop.

The bat family

With more than 1,110 species and more discovered every year, bats make up nearly a quarter of all mammal species. Many scientists divide the large order of bats (Chiroptera) into two subgroups, megabats (large bats) and microbats (small bats). Some scientists, however, no longer separate bats into these two subgroups but simply group bats as Chiroptera.

Fruit bats are megabats, representing about 20 percent of all bat species. Confusingly, some megabats are smaller than some microbats. There are other differences, however, that distinguish the two groups.

How are fruit bats different?

Most microbats feed on insects, especially night-flying insects such as moths. Fruit bats, however, feed on fruit or flowers, and a few species are active by day. Most microbats find their prey and avoid obstacles using echolocation. They produce a stream of high-pitched sounds and listen to

> BAT WINGS CONSIST OF SKIN STRETCHED OVER THE BONES OF THE HAND AND ARM.

the echoes that bounce back from objects. Fruit bats do not use echolocation to nearly the same extent.

Microbats have evolved large, complex ears and leaflike nose flaps to aid echolocation. Fruit bats lack these features. They have foxlike faces with smaller, simpler ears and large eyes. Some large species are known as flying foxes. Fruit bats rely on their excellent eyesight and keen sense of smell to locate food and avoid obstacles as they fly.

Like other bats, the wings of fruit bats consist of skin stretched over the bones of the hand and arm. Fruit bats have sturdy thumbs with a large claw,

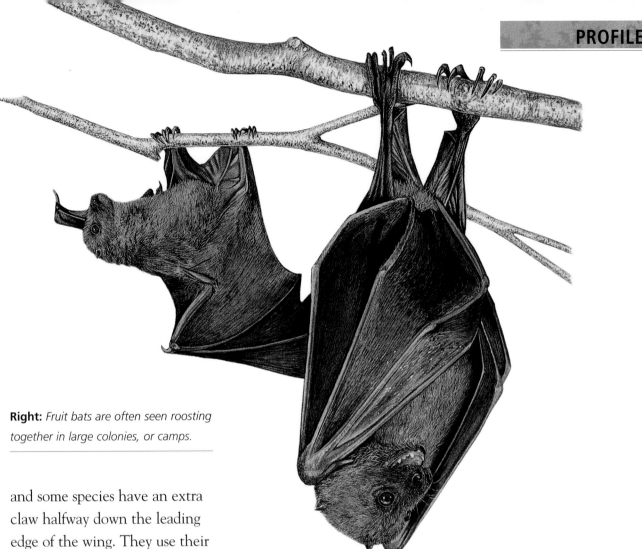

Right: *Fruit bats are often seen roosting together in large colonies, or camps.*

and some species have an extra claw halfway down the leading edge of the wing. They use their claws to climb along branches to reach fruit, and male bats also use them in fights.

Subfamilies

The family of fruit bats, Pteropodidae, is further divided into two subfamilies. The larger subfamily, the true fruit-eating bats, is called Pteropodinae. This group contains around nine-tenths of all fruit bat species. The smaller group, the long-tongued bats, is called Macroglossinae. This group contains about 12 species, which are mostly much smaller than other fruit bats.

DID YOU KNOW?

Ancestors

Bats are thought to have evolved from small tree-living ancestors between 65 and 55 million years ago. That era followed a worldwide catastrophe, probably a meteor hitting Earth. This catastrophe wiped out many other types of animals, including dinosaurs, which had dominated the land for millions of years. Small, warm-blooded early mammals survived the disaster, and in the 10 million years that followed, evolved into many different forms, including bats. Experts believe that all bats evolved from common ancestors because they all have similar DNA (deoxyribonucleic acid; the basic unit of heredity).

Experts believe the ancestors of bats may have resembled flying squirrels, with flaps of skin running down their sides that could be spread to glide between trees. Over millions of years, they evolved the skin wings they now possess.

ANATOMY: Gray-headed flying fox

FREE-TAILED BAT

MOUSE-TAILED BAT

MOUSE-EARED BAT

SHEATH-TAILED BAT

TUBE-NOSED FRUIT BAT

FLYING FOX

Wings
The wing surface is made up of two thin layers of skin. Bones, nerves, and blood vessels are sandwiched between the layers.

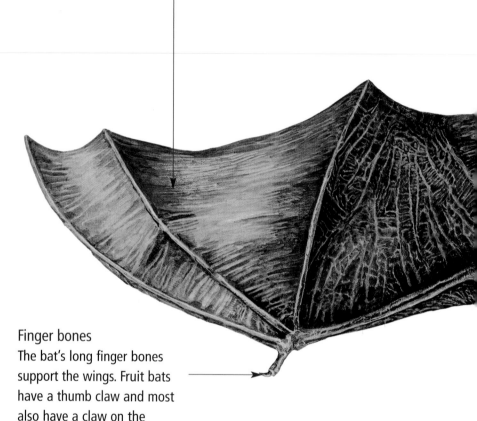

Tails
Fruit bats have tails of various shapes, while some flying foxes have no tail. Rousette fruit bats have a short, stumpy tail. Fruit bats mostly lack the rudderlike tail of microbats that make these smaller, insect-hunting bats agile in flight. However, mouse-tailed bats, which feed on insects, have a long, mobile tail.

Finger bones
The bat's long finger bones support the wings. Fruit bats have a thumb claw and most also have a claw on the second finger. The claws are used for climbing, and male bats use them to fight.

Fruit bat skeleton
Several of the bones in the upper spine are fused. That helps keep the bat's body rigid while flying. The ribs are flattened. That gives the body a streamlined shape and thus reduces drag.

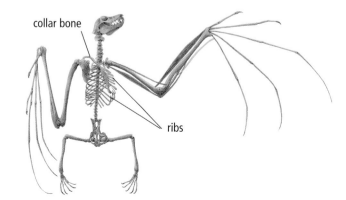

collar bone

ribs

Bones for flying
The bones and muscles of the shoulder are well developed. The large collar bone gives extra strength to the upper body.

Feet
The long claws provide a good grip. A fruit bat can hang upside down by one leg while grooming (cleaning) itself with the other.

Thick fur
The fruit bat's dense fur helps keep it warm. This is especially important for bats that live on high mountains with cold night temperatures.

Large eyes
Fruit bats have excellent night vision. All mammals have special cells at the back of their eyes called rods, which are sensitive to light. In bats' eyes, these cells have fingerlike projections that give them a greater surface area, so they can capture more light.

FACT FILE

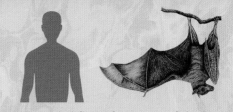

The gray-headed flying fox is one of the largest species of fruit bat with a wingspan of 4 feet (1.2 m).

Gray-headed flying fox

GENUS: *Pteropus*
SPECIES: *poliocephalus*

SIZE

HEAD–BODY LENGTH: male 11.7 inches (30 cm) female 7.8 inches (20 cm)
WEIGHT: Male 2.6 pounds (1.2 kg); female 1.8 pounds (0.8 kg)
WING SPAN: female 2.6 feet (0.8 m)

COLORATION

The upper fur is a grizzled gray, while underneath the coat is much darker, even black in places. The legs are covered in black hairs. There are three white stripes on the head: one between the eyes and one on each cheek. The body is grayish brown to almost black, with a grayish yellow patch on the back between the wings. The ears, wings, and nose are black.

FRUIT BAT SKULL

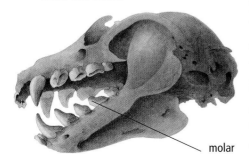

molar

Skulls, jaws, and teeth
The shape of a fruit bat's skull varies from species to species. Those that feed on flowers often have longer, thinner snouts. Teeth also differ according to diet. Back teeth called molars are low and widely spaced with broad crowns.

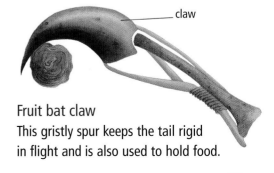

claw

Fruit bat claw
This gristly spur keeps the tail rigid in flight and is also used to hold food.

Hanging loose

Fruit bats need a constant supply of ripe fruit or flowers. For this reason, they live only in tropical and subtropical regions, where fruits and flowers are available all year round. There are no megabat fruit bats in the Americas; they live only from Africa south of the Sahara eastward to the Middle East, and southern Asia to southeast Asia, Australia, and some South Pacific islands. There are, however, some microbats that live in the Americas and that eat fruit.

Wide distribution
The ability to fly is the key to the widespread distribution of fruit bats. Birds are the only other vertebrates (backboned animals) able to achieve powered flight. The earliest remains of fruit bats suggest they may have evolved in southern Europe (where no fruit bats now live) and spread

Left: *Wahlberg's epauletted fruit bat lives in many countries in Africa south of the Sahara desert. After dark, these bats make a distinctive pinging call.*

Distribution

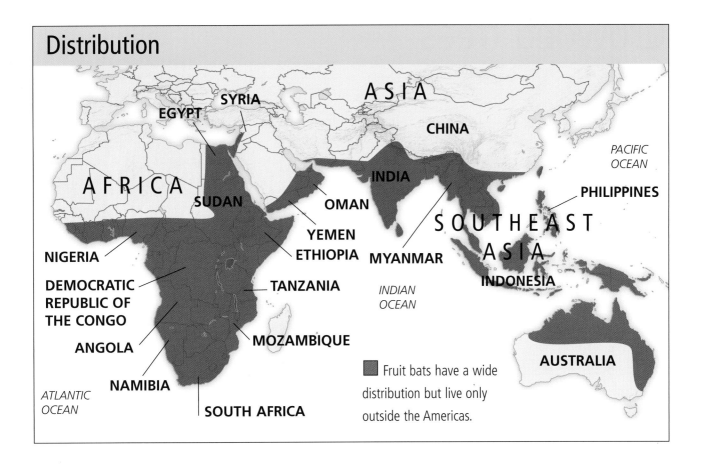

ASIA

EGYPT

SYRIA

CHINA

PACIFIC OCEAN

AFRICA

INDIA

SUDAN

OMAN

PHILIPPINES

YEMEN

S O U T H E A S T

NIGERIA

ETHIOPIA   MYANMAR

A S I A

DEMOCRATIC REPUBLIC OF THE CONGO

TANZANIA

INDONESIA

INDIAN OCEAN

ANGOLA

MOZAMBIQUE

AUSTRALIA

NAMIBIA

ATLANTIC OCEAN

SOUTH AFRICA

■ Fruit bats have a wide distribution but live only outside the Americas.

east and south from there. The power of flight allowed bats to colonize islands fairly close to mainlands, while they may have reached remote islands after being blown out to sea by storms.

Within their range (the total area where they live) fruit bats inhabit a wide variety of habitats, including rain forests, which provide ideal conditions of being warm, wet, and having abundant fruit all year. Fruit bats also live in woodlands, swamps, mountains, islands, and towns and villages, where they roost in homes, barns, and even temples.

A place to rest

Large flying foxes roost in trees. They wrap their wings around themselves to shelter from the wind and rain. Tree roosts are often temporary. Other types of fruit bats make their homes in caves, hollow tree trunks, under roofs or rolled-up banana leaves, or even in old tombs.

DID YOU KNOW?

Need for water

Fruit bats are restricted in their habitats by the need for water. They lose a lot of moisture through the thin skin of their wings, especially when flying, so they always need to be in reach of water. For this reason they do not live in very dry places such as deserts. Bats drink by flying down and dipping their mouths in water. The larger species are less able to maneuver when flying, so they need a fairly large stretch of water to do this. If they fall in, they are strong swimmers. They use their wings to push themselves along the surface. The ability to swim also allows them to grab fruit that has fallen into water.

Crowded trees

Most fruit bats are sociable creatures, feeding in groups and roosting in colonies. Some of the larger species gather in groups of 250,000 animals. African straw-colored bats are one of the most sociable species. During the breeding season they gather in colonies of up to a million bats, but their colonies are smaller at other times of year.

Epauletted fruit bats of Africa roost in groups of between three and 100 bats of both sexes. Other species are less sociable, preferring to live in smaller groups of 10 to 20 bats. Short-nosed fruit bats of southeastern Asia live in groups of between 6 and 12 individuals, with older males living separately. These are the only bats outside the Americas that build shelters, which they make by biting out the middle of a cluster of kitul palm fruit. The bats then nestle in the hollow in the fruit.

Camping out

Many fruit bats do not roost permanently in one place, but move to a different roost each night in search of ripe, soft fruit. Fruit bats are strong fliers and will fly up to 18 miles (29 km) a night to find food. Each night, the bats settle in a temporary roost called a camp. They hang upside down

Above: *Egyptian rousette fruit bats roost in caves, ruined buildings, and tunnels. They are the only fruit bats that use echolocation to find their way.*

while resting. Unlike other bats, fruit bats hold their head at right angles to the body.

Pecking order

A simple hierarchy operates within the bat camp. Large, full-grown males are at the top of the pecking order, with young bats at the bottom.

AMAZING FACTS

• Some large fruit bats fly up to 60 miles (100 km) in a single night.

• One fruit bat landed on the deck of a ship nearly 200 miles (320 km) out to sea at night.

• Male epauletted fruit bats have white hair growing within pouches on their shoulders. These white hairs can be held erect to attract females.

SIDE VIEW

FRONT VIEW

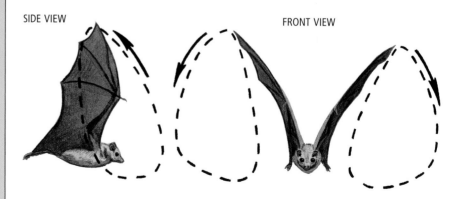

Above: *When a bat is in flight, it raises its wings above its body, then brings them down and flicks them forward before raising them again, in a circular movement.*

The adult males squabble to occupy the best roosting sites. This is especially important in the breeding season. Their squabbles can be noisy, with males screeching, flapping their wings, and baring their sharp fangs. Quarrels may be mended and other ties may be strengthened by grooming. Bats take turns licking and cleaning one another's fur.

Evening feed

Most fruit bats forage for food for about two hours after sunset. They consume about two-thirds of their daily intake of food during this time. At dusk, they take to the air in a mass of flapping wings and swirl around for a few minutes, before they all head off in the same direction to find a feeding site. When a feeding site has

Above: *When fruit bats are not foraging for food, they spend a lot of their time grooming themselves and each other. Grooming keeps their fur clean and free of parasites.*

been located, the bats land and start to eat the fruit and nectar, squabbling over the best feeding perches.

A fruity diet

With their large size, razor-sharp claws, and keen eyesight, it is perhaps surprising that fruit bats generally eat only plants. They occasionally eat insects that have landed on the fruit or flowers they are eating, but do not actively hunt insects. Most species feed mainly on fruit, but in the dry season there may be little fruit, so the bats feed on flowers instead. Long-nosed bats have long tongues and feed on flower pollen and nectar.

The search for ripe fruit and flowering trees governs the lives of fruit bats. If an area is stripped of soft fruit, the bats move on. They find their food mainly by smell. When a tree comes into flower or fruit they can smell it several miles away. Their keen nighttime vision helps them home in on food, and also land safely in the dark.

Fruit bats use their feet to hold on to fruit while eating. Most species do not eat the whole fruit. Instead they squeeze out the juices, squashing the flesh against the ridged bony palate in the roof of their mouth, and chewing

Above: *An Indian short-nosed fruit bat sucks out the flesh from a fruit and spits out the leftover flesh and pulp.*

each mouthful. Only the juice and tiny seeds are swallowed, the skin and pulp are spat out. When feeding on flowers, they use their long tongue to collect pollen and nectar.

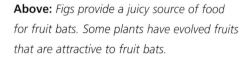

Above: *Figs provide a juicy source of food for fruit bats. Some plants have evolved fruits that are attractive to fruit bats.*

Helping plants

Fruit bats help trees and flowering plants reproduce by spreading pollen and seeds. While a bat feeds on flowers, some of the pollen rubs off on its fur, to be transferred to the next flower it visits. This pollinates the second flower, allowing the plant to produce fruit and seeds. Bats feeding on fruit spit out large seeds, which fall to the ground where they may sprout. Small seeds are swallowed and pass right through the bat's digestive system. Eventually they pass out in the animal's dung, or guano, to sprout in a different part of the forest.

COMPETITORS

Many other kinds of animals feed on fruit or flowers. These animals include:

GIBBON (family Hylobatidae)
Gibbons feed on ripe fruit in the forests of Southeast Asia. These agile apes swing between trees using their long arms.

ORANGUTAN (*Pongo pygmaeus*)
Orangutans are apes that live in the rain forests of Borneo and Sumatra where they feed mostly on fruit.

HORNBILL (family Bucerotidae)
Birds called hornbills feed mainly on fruit. The great Indian hornbill lives in southern Asia.

GLIDER (family Petauridae)
In Australia and New Guinea, small marsupials called gliders feed on flower pollen and nectar— the diet of some long-tongued bats.

Below: *The nectar-eating fruit bat moves from flower to flower eating nectar. As it does so, pollen rubs off on its body and the bat transfers the pollen to other plants.*

central nervous
system develops

limb buds develop

wings begin to develop

fetus nears term

Noisy courtship

The breeding habits of fruit bats vary. Many of the larger species breed just once a year. Some species that dwell in forests with seasonal rainfall mate in the dry season. This ensures that the offspring are born during the wet season.

Courtship and mating

Courting bats are often noisy. The male gray-headed flying fox lays claim to a branch on the roost. He uses his

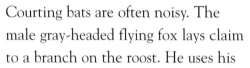

Left: *The development of the fetus inside a bat's uterus takes from 45 days for small bats to six months for larger species.*

extra claw to defend his territory against rivals. As dusk falls he flaps his large wings, making short, screechlike barks. The noise attracts the females, who choose the males with the biggest wings and loudest barks to mate with.

Hammer-headed fruit bats breed twice yearly. The males gather at breeding sites called leks. The adult males spread out, and begin making loud, regular honking sounds while flapping their wings furiously. Their calls are amplified by their hammer-shaped snouts and large voice boxes. The female bats are very choosy. They hover in front of the males, who increase their rate of honking and flapping. After several visits they finally land on a male, and mating takes place.

Birth and growing up

Fruit bats usually give birth to a single offspring, but sometimes twins. Gestation times are long, up to six months in the largest species. This is a long time for a relatively small mammal. The babies are born large and well developed, with furry coats and open eyes. The newborn bat clings tightly to its mother's fur and suckles her milk. The female carries her heavy baby with her while searching for food, but leaves it hanging from a nearby branch while she feeds.

Indian flying fox

BREEDING: July–October
GESTATION: 140–150 days
LITTER SIZE: 1
WEIGHT AT BIRTH: 7–10 ounces (198–283 g)
EYES OPEN: At birth
FIRST FLIGHT: 2–3 months
WEANED: 5 months
INDEPENDENT: 6–8 months
REACH BREEDING AGE: 18–24 months
LIFESPAN: 12–15 years in the wild, up to 31 years in captivity

Egyptian rousette fruit bat

BREEDING: June–September
GESTATION: 110–130 days
LITTER SIZE: 1 or 2
WEIGHT AT BIRTH: 1–1.4 ounces (28–40 g)
EYES OPEN: At birth
FIRST FLIGHT: 4–5 months
WEANED: 4 months
INDEPENDENT: 5 months females; 15 months males
REACH BREEDING AGE: 18–24 months
LIFESPAN: 11–14 years in the wild, up to 23 years in captivity

Young fruit bats grow quickly, flapping their wings while hanging upside down, which strengthens their flight muscles. When ready to fly, they simply let go. If they hit the ground they climb back up and try again. They continue to drink their mother's milk for another month or so. At about eight months old, young females set up a roost of their own. Young males stay with their mother for up to two years. Young bats reach breeding age at any time between six months and two years old.

BABY BATS: Following a noisy courtship, mating occurs. The gestation period for fruit bats can be as long as six months, which is a very long time for animals of this size. Baby fruit bats are born large, alert, and with their eyes open. These qualities help the baby bat survive.

The life of a fruit bat

TAKING TO THE AIR: The offspring of larger fruit bats take their first flight at about three months. During this time, however, they continue to suckle.

LEFT HANGING AROUND: Mothers cannot eat and look after their offspring at the same time. Instead, they leave their young hanging on a branch near the feeding area.

Troubled times

Fruit bats are one of the most common mammals in many tropical regions, particularly on forested islands. However, their numbers are falling everywhere, and some species are facing extinction. Natural disasters such as drought, storms, and even volcanic eruptions have harmed some species and their habitats, but the main problems are caused by people.

Hunting

Hunting is a serious threat in many regions. For thousands of years, local people have hunted bats for food. However, modern methods such as using rifles have made hunting all too easy. On some islands, such as Guam in the Philippines, people eat fruit bats. Several species, including the Guam flying fox, have been hunted to extinction, and other local bats are threatened.

Habitat loss

As the population grows throughout the tropics, so forests and woodlands where fruit bats live are cut down to provide fuel or timber, or cleared to build new roads and towns. Quarrying and mining also harm the habitats of some species, such as the dawn fruit bat of Malaysia.

Wild habitats are also being replaced by new farms and plantations, on which crops

Location

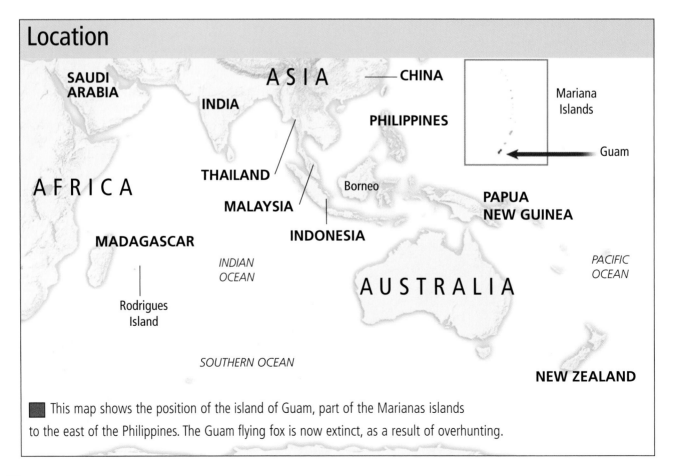

This map shows the position of the island of Guam, part of the Marianas islands to the east of the Philippines. The Guam flying fox is now extinct, as a result of overhunting.

are grown for food or profit. Plantations of fruit trees such as bananas provide unnatural concentrations of food that attract fruit bats, but that leads to clashes with farmers. When local people find their crops destroyed by bats, they retaliate by shooting or poisoning the culprits. In many areas, the decline of fruit bats has had serious results for forests and woodlands because the bats are no longer there to pollinate trees and spread their seeds.

Conservation

Some species of bats are now legally protected, but they are still killed illegally. Captive breeding projects in zoos are helping to save endangered species such as the Rodrigues fruit bat of Rodrigues Island, east of Mauritius in the Indian Ocean. The habitats of some endangered bats, including some island species, are now protected as preserves or national parks.

CHECK THESE OUT

RELATIVES: • Bats, small • Leaf-nosed bats • Vesper bats
COMPETITORS: • Gibbons • Galagos and relatives

Right: *The destruction of farmland and forests for their timber and for road building poses a serious threat to many fruit bat species.*

At risk

The chart shows how the International Union for the Conservation of Nature (IUCN) defines the threat to fruit bats:

PANAY GIANT FRUIT BAT; PHILIPPINE BARE-BACKED FRUIT BAT; DUSKY, OKINAWA, PALAU, AND GUAM FLYING FOXES	*Extinct*
BULMER'S FRUIT BAT; ALDABRA, CHUUK, BONIN, MORTLOCK, AND RODRIGUES FLYING FOXES	*Critically endangered*
POHLE'S FRUIT BAT; RYUKYU, NICOBAR, AND MARIANAS FLYING FOXES	*Endangered*

Endangered means that the species faces a very high risk of extinction in the wild. *Critically endangered* means that the species faces an extremely high risk of extinction. *Extinct* means that the last individual has died.

HORSES
AND ASSES

Wild horses once roamed freely over much of Europe and Asia. Now, herds of horses live only in parts of the United States and Australia. These horses, called mustangs and brumbies, are feral animals, the descendants of domestic horses that have returned to the wild.

Below: *A herd of Przewalski's horses gallops across the grasslands near the Altai mountains in Mongolia. These wild horses, discovered only in the nineteenth century, are extinct in the wild but they have been reintroduced to their native habitat.*

Built for Speed

H orses, zebras, and asses are equids—members of a small family, Equidae, within the larger group of odd-toed ungulates (hoofed mammals that make up the order Perissodactyla). They belong to the genus *Equus*. This chapter examines the natural history of horses and asses. Zoologists know a lot about the evolution of equids because there have been so many fossil discoveries. The earliest ancestor of present-day equids, known as *Hyracotherium*, appeared about 60 million years ago.

Above: *Asiatic asses are the most horselike of the asses. They have a sandy brown winter coat with white undersides and a broad black dorsal stripe. In summer, the coat is reddish brown.*

RELATIVES

Horses and asses are members of the order Perissodactyla—ungulates (hoofed mammals) with a single toe on each foot. Close relatives include:

RHINOCEROS (family Rhinocerotidae)
These three-toed ungulates are the second-largest terrestrial mammals, after elephants. Depending on the species, either one or two horns project from the end of the snout of the rhinoceros.

TAPIR (family Tapiridae)
Tapirs have been around for more than 50 million years. Tapirs look much like their early ancestors, which form an evolutionary link between insectivores and modern ungulates.

ZEBRA (family Equidae)
Zebras are members of the same family as horses and asses. The zebra's distinctive stripes may act as camouflage against predation. Recent research suggests the stripes may also stimulate contact between individuals in the herd.

Between 38 and 25 million years ago, equids died out in Europe and Asia, but the evolution of the equid family continued in North America. Later, horses repopulated Europe and Asia by crossing land bridges that existed then between the continents.

One-toed horses

Fossil evidence suggests that the first true one-toed horse, *Pliohippus*, appeared fewer than five million years ago. Fossil remains were found in the United States, but this species probably first appeared in Europe and Asia. *Pliohippus* is thought to be the direct ancestor of members of the genus *Equus*, which includes all modern horses and asses.

This early, primitive, horselike mammal was about the same size as a lamb and had three toes on the forefeet and four toes on each hind foot.

Over time, the limbs of these early equids grew proportionally longer and more slender, and the number of toes on each foot reduced from three to one. The body became larger, with a straight spine, and the teeth gradually changed to suit a grazing lifestyle.

Below: *Przewalski's horse was discovered by Russian explorer Nikolai Przewalski (1839–1888). This equid has short legs and a stocky body.*

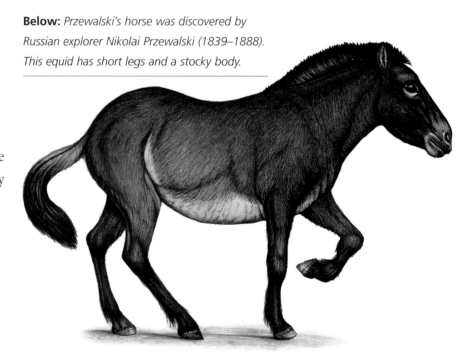

DID YOU KNOW?

Ancestors

The early ancestors of present-day equids had three or four toes on each foot. With no defensive weaponry, such as claws or horns, these timid ungulates probably hid from predators among the dense vegetation of their rain-forest habitat. When equids moved into the open grasslands, they evolved longer limbs to outpace predators. The outer toes became smaller and smaller until they had disappeared, while the central toe became larger. The single hoof comes from a modified nail and forms a hard pad. A soft, V-shaped growth on the sole of the foot, called the frog, has also developed to absorb the impact of the legs as the horse gallops.

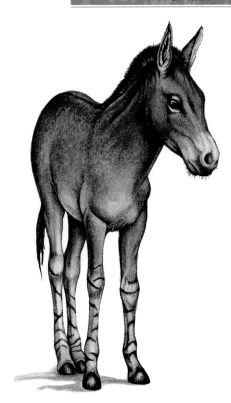

Present-day horses and asses

Modern equids are built for speed, with long legs and slender, muscular bodies. Asses are generally smaller and stockier than horses. Both males and females have long, straight necks with coarse manes running along the neck. Some individuals have a bunch of hair between the ears, called a forelock. The head is large, and the ears lie flat or stand erect to indicate what sort of mood the horse is in.

The color of the coat varies among species, but it tends to match the color of the environment in which the species lives. For example, Przewalski's horse and both the African and Asiatic asses have gray to sandy brown coats, with stripes that vary between the species.

All horses have excellent hearing and color vision. They are highly social animals and live in groups.

Above: *An African wild ass. These equids are native to Sudan, Ethiopia, and Somalia. They have been bred for centuries as working animals.*

Right: *The Asiatic wild ass is slightly larger than the African ass. In summer, the coat is reddish brown, becoming lighter brown in the winter. There is a black stripe along the back and the underside is white.*

ANATOMY: Przewalski's horse

Odor detection
A stallion (male horse) draws back its lips in a reaction called the flehmen response. This action allows the stallion to breath in scents left by other horses and analyse them using a structure called the vomeronasal pouch, which is located on the roof of the mouth. This behavior is particularly common when a stallion smells the urine of a mare (female horse) to find out if she is ready to mate.

Foot
Each foot has a single toe that projects the horny outer hoof—a modified nail. The hoof adds length to the limb and increases the horse's ability to run at high speeds.

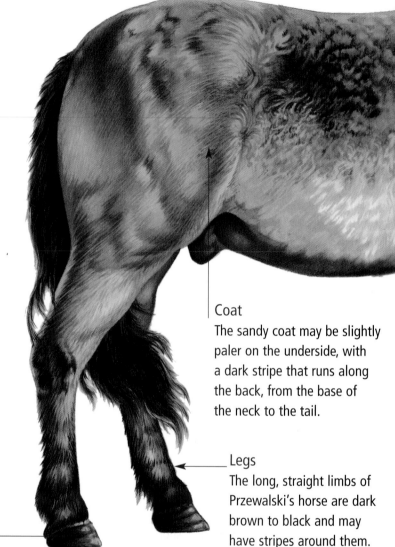

Coat
The sandy coat may be slightly paler on the underside, with a dark stripe that runs along the back, from the base of the neck to the tail.

Legs
The long, straight limbs of Przewalski's horse are dark brown to black and may have stripes around them.

Skeleton
The long, straight spine of the horse is built for speed. Just like in other mammals, it consists of five distinct sections from neck to tail: the cervical, dorsal, lumbar, sacral, and caudal regions.

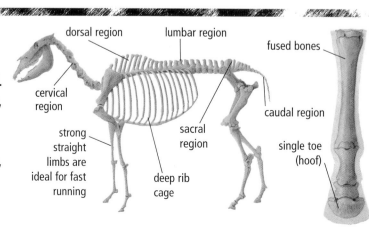

dorsal region

lumbar region

cervical region

strong straight limbs are ideal for fast running

deep rib cage

sacral region

caudal region

fused bones

single toe (hoof)

The feet
The foot bones in both the forelimbs and hind limbs are fused, which allows the horse to twist and turn safely at high speed.

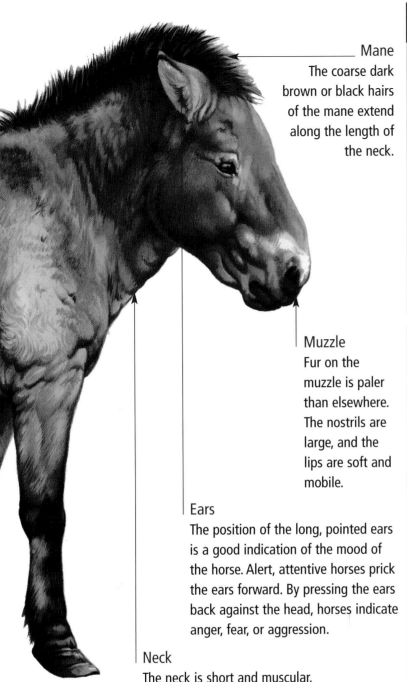

Mane
The coarse dark brown or black hairs of the mane extend along the length of the neck.

Muzzle
Fur on the muzzle is paler than elsewhere. The nostrils are large, and the lips are soft and mobile.

Ears
The position of the long, pointed ears is a good indication of the mood of the horse. Alert, attentive horses prick the ears forward. By pressing the ears back against the head, horses indicate anger, fear, or aggression.

Neck
The neck is short and muscular.

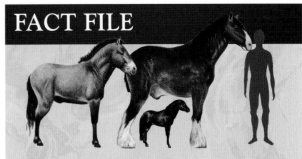
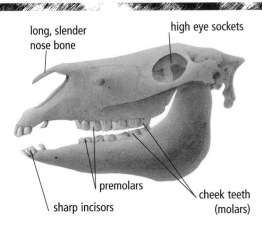

long, slender nose bone

high eye sockets

sharp incisors

premolars

cheek teeth (molars)

The skull
The eye sockets are set high on the long skull and well behind the cheek teeth. This means that chewing action does not place pressure on the horse's eyes.

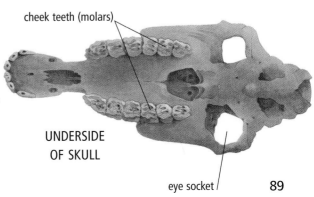

cheek teeth (molars)

UNDERSIDE OF SKULL

eye socket

89

Cold tundra to dry desert

Most feral (wild) horses inhabit grasslands in a range of different climates. Przewalski's horse was discovered on the steppes (treeless plains) of Mongolia, where the Altai mountains meet the Gobi desert.

During the spring and summer, these horses roamed over the mountain slopes up to an altitude of about 8,000 feet (2,440 m), descending to about 5,000 feet (1,525 m) in the fall. Their range also extended into the desert, where they grazed on the sparse vegetation.

Desert breeds

Many breeds have long thrived in desert regions. The Arab, one of the oldest surviving breeds, was tamed by tribespeople of the Arabian deserts thousands of years ago. The supreme stamina of the Arabian horse results from its ability to survive in such an inhospitable environment. Other desert-dwelling breeds include the mustang of the United States and the brumby of Australia.

Colder climates

Similarly, many horses have made their homes in the cold tundra (frozen, treeless plains) of the northern hemisphere. Many breeds, such as the Shetland pony, are thought to be descendants of hardy breeds from Scandinavia. The Shetland pony has lived on the remote Shetland Islands off the coast of mainland Scotland for 10,000 years or more. This small breed feeds on grass, lichen, and tree bark and may even scavenge on the beach for dead fish.

Moors and marshes

Many familiar pony breeds, such as Dales, Dartmoor, Exmoor, Fells, and Connemara,

---

DESERT-DWELLING BREEDS INCLUDE THE MUSTANG OF THE UNITED STATES AND THE BRUMBY OF AUSTRALIA.

---

still roam wild on the moors of Britain and Ireland. However, people own these animals, and they are rounded up from time to time. Few purebred ponies now exist on the moors because of interbreeding among the different breeds. Herds of semiwild horses also live in the salt marshes of the Camargue in southern France.

Wild asses

The African wild ass was once widespread in the remote, rocky deserts of Africa and the Arabian Peninsula. Asiatic wild asses were also common

AMAZING FACTS

- Horses and ponies are defined by the height at the withers (the point where the shoulders join the neck). A pony measures no more than 4.6 feet (1.4 m) at the withers; above this height, it is called a horse. Przewalski's horse is an exception to this rule.
- Domestic horses and ponies are measured in units called hands. One hand is equal to 4 inches (10 cm).
- The Ariegeois is a horse native to southwestern France. This hardy breed lives high in the Pyrenees mountains, a natural border between France and Spain.

in similar desert habitats and on the steppes and salt flats of central Asia. Semiwild asses still live in parts of eastern Africa and from Iran to China in Asia. Asiatic wild asses live only in protected preserves in China, India, Iran, and Turkmenistan. Like the larger horses, asses have been taken to regions far from their native habitat—the donkey, for example, originates from the African wild ass.

Below: *Asiatic wild asses. Scattered populations live throughout their range in Syria, Iran, northern India, and Tibet. Thy are the most horselike asses, with broad, round hooves.*

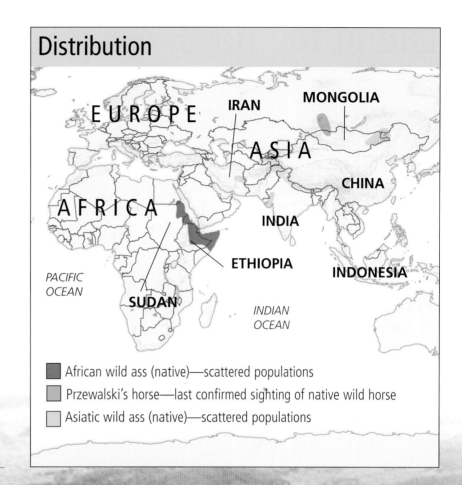

Distribution

EUROPE

IRAN

MONGOLIA

ASIA

CHINA

AFRICA

INDIA

ETHIOPIA

INDONESIA

PACIFIC OCEAN

SUDAN

INDIAN OCEAN

■ African wild ass (native)—scattered populations
■ Przewalski's horse—last confirmed sighting of native wild horse
■ Asiatic wild ass (native)—scattered populations

Life in the herd

All equids naturally herd, whether in the wild or in a stable. Feral or semiwild horses live in small groups, grazing alone but calling to each other with a soft whinny. Within the herd, equids often stand head to tail, gently nibbling the hindquarters of the horse in front to remove dead skin and parasites and keeping watch for predators. The tail of each horse also brushes away flies from the face of its partner.

Social structure

One stallion (male) dominates each small herd. The herd is made up of a few mares—a group called a harem—and their foals (young offspring). The herd roams within a home range, which is limited in size to the availability of grazing pastures and water. There is a strict pecking order for both sexes, but life within the herd is usually peaceful.

The home ranges of different herds often overlap without too much conflict. Fights between

Above: *Fighting stallions kick and bite each other. The winner becomes the dominant male.*

stallions occur when there is a challenge for leadership of the herd. The fights range from threatening facial gestures to violent kicks and bites. Stallions have large, spade-shaped canines that can result in a nasty nip. These fights are rare, however, and it is unusual for a dominant stallion to lose control of his herd. Most young stallions form harems by stealing young mares from herds of dominant stallions.

Herding behavior of asses

The herds of the African and Asiatic wild asses are much looser than those of horses. Mature males establish a territory, which may cover up to 9 square miles (23 sq km). The dominant male usually allows junior males to stay nearby but drives all males from his territory during the breeding season.

Females and young males often roam in large, unstable herds, which form and disband in the same day. Although these horses exhibit some of the herding behavior of stable groups, there is little or no grooming and communication characteristic of horses. Often, these unstable groups wander through the territory of a dominant male, which mates with receptive females.

Above: *A herd of mares watches the stallions fighting from a safe distance.*

DID YOU KNOW?

Horse whisperers

Horses communicate in many different ways. Members of a herd may greet each other by calling softly and touching muzzles. Individuals of lower social rank then lower their head and chew gently with an open mouth. Grazing horses often blow softly to indicate contentment, and stallions squeal during fights over mares. Over longer distances, horses communicate using a loud whinny. Horses also snort when they feel threatened and may flatten their ears against the head.

Groups of grazers

Above: *A family herd of African wild asses graze on scrubland in Somalia. Somalian wild asses have a grayish coat with a dark stripe along the back, white bellies, and dark leg bands.*

The main source of food for all equids is grass. Horses and asses are large animals that need to eat a lot of grass to survive. Horses graze for much of the day. In times of good grass growth, horses may spend around 60 percent of their time grazing. As the vegetation becomes more sparse, and the grass less nutritious, they may spend a longer time grazing. In the fall and winter, for example, up to 80 percent of the day is spent grazing and wandering in search of new pastures.

Equids can survive in areas where the vegetation is so thin that it would seem impossible for such large mammals to live. They do so by eating whatever they can find—buds, fruits, leaves, roots, twigs, tree bark, and lichen. They use their sensitive, mobile lips to gather

Digestion inside a horse

Some herbivorous (plant-eating) mammals are ruminants—they chew their tough, fibrous plant food more than once before it is fully digested. Herbivores, such as cows, have four large stomach chambers (one of which is called the rumen) in which to break down their food. The digestive system of the horse is much simpler. Microorganisms break down the plant material in part of the colon (large gut) called the cecum. Horses do not fully digest their food and they need to eat a lot more of it to get all the nutrients they need.

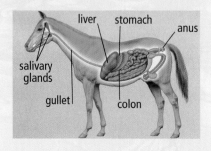

liver stomach anus
salivary glands
gullet colon

up the food before tearing it off between strong upper and lower incisors (cutting teeth).

Foraging for food and water

Wild asses live in areas that may lack vegetation rich in nutrients. The African wild ass usually forages at dawn and late afternoon, resting in the shade during the midday heat. These hardy animals eat grass, sedges, other herbaceous plants, and low-level shrubs. Asiatic wild asses also graze on grass and browse on low-lying succulents, but they can survive on straw by eating vast quantities of it

Asses can live for long periods without water. However, a particularly thirsty animal will roam widely in search of

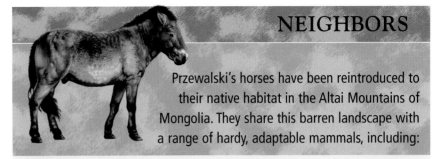

NEIGHBORS

Przewalski's horses have been reintroduced to their native habitat in the Altai Mountains of Mongolia. They share this barren landscape with a range of hardy, adaptable mammals, including:

JERBOA (family Dipodidae)
These burrowing rodents move about by hopping, using their long ears as radiators to keep cool. In extreme heat, jerboas rest in their burrows.

DAURIAN PIKA (Ochotona dauurica)
These rabbitlike mountain dwellers spend much of the day basking on rocky outcrops.

BACTRIAN CAMEL (Camelus bactrianus)
This even-toed ungulate still roams wild in the Gobi Altai, using its distinctive humps as fat storage.

GOITERED GAZELLE (Gazella subgutturosa)
There are relatively few goitered gazelles left in the Gobi region. This species has been hunted for food and sport.

Above: *A Shetland pony scrapes away the snow to find grass. These hardy grazers have to survive harsh, cold winters when there is little food to eat.*

a watering hole, especially during hot summers. Among the horses, Przewalski's horse can survive without water for longer periods than its cousins.

Always on the lookout

With its neck stooped toward the ground, a horse may seem unaware of its surroundings. As a horse grazes, however, it keeps watch on objects some distance away.

Horses also constantly flick their ears back and forth to listen for danger.

Dominant breeders

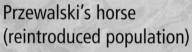orses and asses breed throughout the year, but feral (wild) mares give birth only when there is enough grass on which to feed. For the feral mustangs of the United States and reintroduced populations of Przewalski's horse in Mongolia, the peak time for births is between April and June.

Przewalski's horse (reintroduced population)

BREEDING SEASON: Between April and June

GESTATION: About 335 days

NUMBER OF YOUNG: 1

AGE AT SEXUAL MATURITY: Males 4–5 years; females 3–4 years

LIFE SPAN: Up to 34 years

African wild ass

BREEDING SEASON: Mating may occur all year round; births usually take place in the wet season

GESTATION: 1 year

NUMBER OF YOUNG: 1

AGE AT SEXUAL MATURITY: Males 2–3 years; females 1–2 years

LIFE SPAN: Maximum 47 years (captive animals)

Asiatic wild ass

BREEDING SEASON: Between April and October

GESTATION: 330 days on average

NUMBER OF YOUNG: 1

AGE AT SEXUAL MATURITY: Males 2–3 years; females 1–2 years

LIFE SPAN: Maximum 35 years (captive individuals)

STALLION CONTESTS: Young horses leave the herd when they are ready to mate. Mares may be lured from the herd by young stallions, which form bachelor groups until they are ready to form a harem of their own. Violent fights occasionally break out between stallions, which contest for the right to mate with receptive mares.

The life of a feral horse

STAYING CLOSE: When the herd is on the move, the foal stays at its mother's side. When threatened, members of the herd close around the foals to protect them.

A QUIET BIRTH: The mare gives birth in a sheltered spot, well away from the rest of the herd.

BACK TOGETHER AGAIN: The mare and foal rejoin the herd soon after the birth. Foals play with others in the group, while the mares graze nearby.

DID YOU KNOW?

Foals can walk within a few hours of birth. Their long legs help them keep up with the herd when fleeing from predators. The long bones and muscles of its legs take about two years to develop fully. Before this time, the young horse must take care not to run too fast for too long because there is a high risk that it will damage its underdeveloped leg bones.

For African and Asiatic wild asses, most foals are born to match the time of the year when there is most food—during the wet season for African asses and between April and late October for Asiatic asses.

Competition for mares

The dominant stallion (highest-ranking male) mates with his harem—the mares (females) in his herd—and fights off the attentions of rival stallions. The stallion checks the mare's urine to see if she is ready to mate. The gestation period varies for different horses and asses. Przewalski's horse gives birth around 335 days after mating; asses gestate for between 330 and 360 days. Domestic breeds give birth between 315 and 385 days after mating.

Newborn foals

Mares give birth away from the herd. With its eyes open and ears pricked, the newborn foal can stand within a few minutes. Soon after, the foal can walk and then run (see the box below). Foals start to cut their first teeth after about 10 days but only start to graze after six weeks. They continue to suckle milk for up to a year. It takes about six months to develop a full set of milk teeth. The foal's milk teeth are replaced by adult incisors by the time the young horse is five or six years old.

Ready to breed

Young horses usually leave the herd when they are ready to mate for the first time. The young mares usually join the herds of a nearby stallion, while young stallions group together in small numbers until they form harems of their own.

Doubt for wild horses

Horses and asses have a long history of association with people. For thousands of years, these hardy mammals have been used to help farmers cultivate the land and carry people and their belongings from place to place. Despite this close relationship, and the huge number of domestic breeds of horses in existence, the future of wild horses and asses is in doubt.

Above: *Australian brumbies canter across the plains. It is hard to predict whether they have a long-term future.*

Asses in the wild

The Asiatic wild ass was once common across vast areas of Eurasia. It roamed in huge herds from Palestine to the Gobi Desert of Mongolia. For thousands of years, the Asiatic wild ass has been captured and domesticated as well as hunted for food and leather. By the early eighteenth century, wild herds were pushed out of western Russia and central Asia as people developed the land. By the beginning of the twentieth century, there were no recorded herds left in

DID YOU KNOW?

Giant colony

Przewalski's horse is named for Russian explorer Colonel Nikolai Przewalski, who discovered the species in the Gobi Altai region of Mongolia in the 1870s. The discovery attracted enormous interest in the western world, and many zoos paid vast amounts of money to animal collectors to stock the new species. In subsequent years, the population of wild Przewalski's horses disappeared as agriculture spread across the grasslands of Mongolia. The last confirmed sighting in the wild came in 1968. Fortunately, it seems that the captive population has saved the species from complete extinction.

THEN AND NOW

This map shows the last sighting and former distribution of Przewalski's horse.

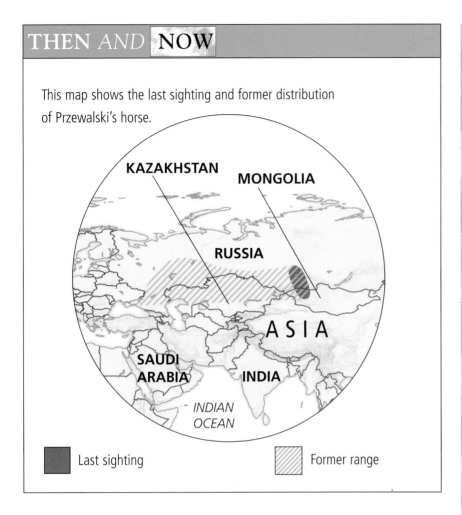

KAZAKHSTAN

MONGOLIA

RUSSIA

A S I A

SAUDI ARABIA

INDIA

INDIAN OCEAN

■ Last sighting   ▨ Former range

At risk

The International Union for the Conservation of Nature (IUCN) lists the following species of horses and asses in the *Red List of Threatened Species*:

AFRICAN WILD ASS	*Critically endangered*
ASIATIC WILD ASS	*Vulnerable*
PRZEWALSKI'S HORSE	*Extinct in the wild*

Extinct in the wild means that the species is known to survive only in captivity or as a naturalized population well outside its past range. *Critically endangered* means that the species faces an extremely high risk of extinction in the wild in the immediate future. *Vulnerable* means that the species faces a high risk of extinction in the wild in the near future.

Kazakhstan. There are probably thousands of truly wild Asiatic asses, which roam in protected reserves in China, India, Iran, and Turkmenistan.

African wild asses have fared less well and may be extinct in the wild in many parts of their former range. At best, fewer than 1,000 animals may exist in pockets of eastern Africa.

Feral horses

The mustangs of the North American prairies and the Australian brumbies are perhaps the best known feral breeds. Both populations are the descendants of domestic horses brought into the continents by explorers and settlers. When the original horses escaped, only the hardiest individuals survived and bred in the wild. Over the centuries, vast populations of feral horses roamed in the wilds of both continents.

During the twentieth century, however, the feral horses of America and Australia suffered at the hands of farmers and developers, who blamed

them for grazing fields set aside for domestic stock. To control the threat, huge numbers of feral horses were killed and sold for meat. By the end of the 1970s, few brumbies and mustangs existed in the wild.

CHECK THESE OUT

RELATIVES: • Rhinoceroses • Zebras

KILLER WHALES

The killer whale, or orca, is the largest member of the dolphin family. This air-breathing mammal swims and hunts in all the world's oceans. Orcas eat almost any medium to large prey they can overpower, but not people.

Below: *A killer whale jumps clear of the ocean's surface in an action called breaching.*

- **COMMON NAME:** Killer whale, or orca
- **SCIENTIFIC NAME:** *Orcinus orca*
- **CLOSELY RELATED SPECIES:** The false killer whale is slightly smaller than the killer whale, and the pygmy killer whale is smaller still.
- **HABITAT:** The surface waters of any ocean, but usually prefer cooler, shallower waters
- **RANGE:** Patchy distribution, from polar to tropical waters
- **APPEARANCE:** The largest member of the dolphin family, the killer whale is boldly marked in black, white, and shades of gray; bluntish head with sleek, muscular body. The dorsal (back) fin is very tall, particularly in males. The back and flanks are black with a dark gray saddle behind the dorsal fin. The underside is white. There is a bold white patch behind both eyes.

The Clever Killer

The killer whale has bold markings and a playful nature. It lives in family groups called pods and is one of nature's most deadly killers. Killer whales hunting in family groups take any prey, from squid and fish the size of herring, to other whales that are much bigger than themselves. Off the west coast of North America, biologists have filmed killer whales forcing themselves between a gray whale mother and her calf and then attacking and eating the calf. Killer whales pose little or no threat to people, however.

These intelligent and cooperative animals communicate with each other

Above: *This killer whale is spy-hopping. It rises straight up out of the water to see what is happening above the surface.*

DID YOU KNOW?

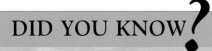

All whales, dolphins, and porpoises are probably descended from land-living carnivorous (meat-eating) mammals called mesonychids. These creatures lived more than 60 million years ago and looked like large wolves, but with hooved feet. Over millions of years, some of these mammals began to walk and swim in shallow water. Among the earliest of these creatures, dating from about 50 million years ago, was *Ambulocetus*. It looked like a cross between a hairy crocodile and a giant otter. It had short legs, a long tail used as a paddle, and a large mouth well armed with teeth. By 30 million years ago, these creatures had evolved into forms recognizable as toothed whales. They had lost almost all traces of fur, their forelimbs were flippers, and their hind limbs had almost disappeared. The tail was now stretched into horizontal flukes (flat paddles) and the nostrils had moved to the top of the head to form a blowhole. All these changes allowed the creatures to better swim and breathe in water.

Below: *The largest and most common of the killer whales are also called great killer whales, or orcas. They are instantly recognizable by their striking black-and-white coloration and large dorsal (back) fin.*

using an array of sounds and visual signals as they go about their lives hunting, playing, courting, breeding, and raising their young.

There are three species of killer whales. The most familiar species is simply called the killer whale, or orca. It is by far the largest member of the dolphin family. Big males can reach about 30 feet (9 m) long and weigh 9 tons (8 metric tons), as much as two African elephants. The two smaller species of killer whales are the false killer whale, which reaches about 2 tons, and the much smaller pygmy killer whale, which grows to a maximum size of 375 pounds (170 kg).

The killer whale—like all whales, dolphins, and porpoises—is a cetacean. It is a member of the order (major group) Cetacea. All cetaceans are whales. This order is split into toothed whales and baleen whales. About 70 species are toothed whales, or odontocetes, and about 14 species are baleen whales, or mysticetes.

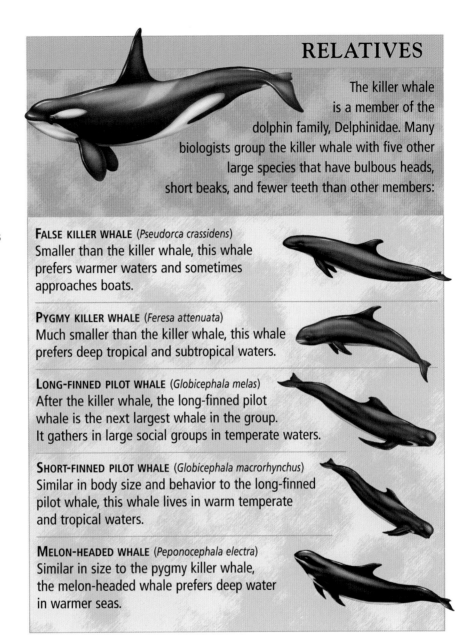

RELATIVES

The killer whale is a member of the dolphin family, Delphinidae. Many biologists group the killer whale with five other large species that have bulbous heads, short beaks, and fewer teeth than other members:

FALSE KILLER WHALE (*Pseudorca crassidens*)
Smaller than the killer whale, this whale prefers warmer waters and sometimes approaches boats.

PYGMY KILLER WHALE (*Feresa attenuata*)
Much smaller than the killer whale, this whale prefers deep tropical and subtropical waters.

LONG-FINNED PILOT WHALE (*Globicephala melas*)
After the killer whale, the long-finned pilot whale is the next largest whale in the group. It gathers in large social groups in temperate waters.

SHORT-FINNED PILOT WHALE (*Globicephala macrorhynchus*)
Similar in body size and behavior to the long-finned pilot whale, this whale lives in warm temperate and tropical waters.

MELON-HEADED WHALE (*Peponocephala electra*)
Similar in size to the pygmy killer whale, the melon-headed whale prefers deep water in warmer seas.

Baleen whales do not have teeth but instead strain seawater for fish, squid, or small shrimplike organisms. They use a comblike structure, like a set of bristles inside the mouth, called a baleen. The very largest whales, such as blue whales, fin whales, and humpback whales, are baleen whales.

Toothed whales include sperm whales, beaked whales, dolphins, and porpoises. These whales have various numbers of teeth, ranging from the narwhal and the beluga, which have only one or two teeth, to some dolphins that have more than 100 teeth. Toothed whales range in size from sperm whales, at 60 feet (18 m) long,

to the vaquita, a small porpoise, at 5 feet (1.5 m) that lives in the Gulf of California.

Most people call smaller toothed whales either dolphins or porpoises. Dolphins, most of which are members of the family Delphinidae, have peglike teeth, while porpoises (family Phocoenidae) have chisel-shaped teeth.

ANATOMY: Killer whale

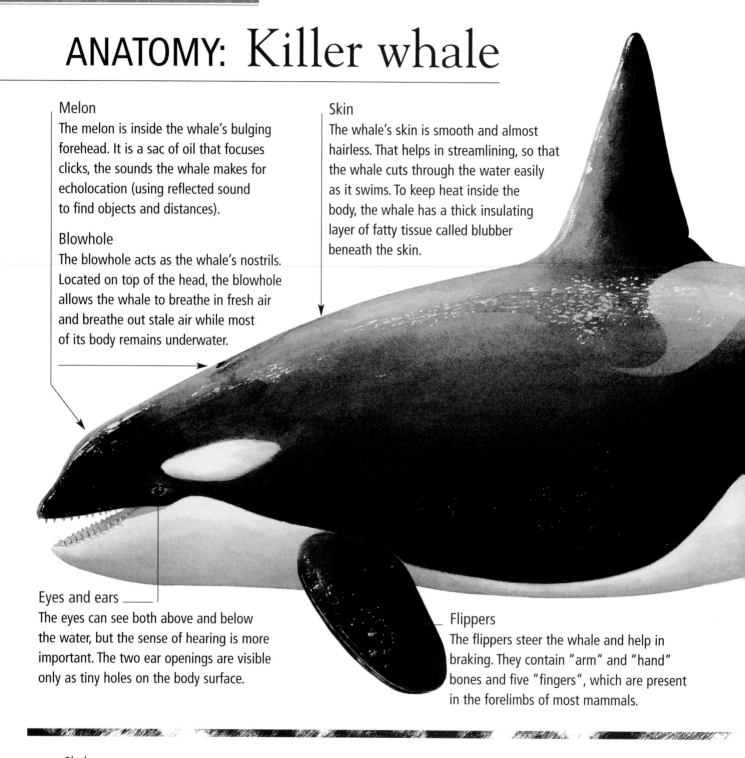

Melon
The melon is inside the whale's bulging forehead. It is a sac of oil that focuses clicks, the sounds the whale makes for echolocation (using reflected sound to find objects and distances).

Blowhole
The blowhole acts as the whale's nostrils. Located on top of the head, the blowhole allows the whale to breathe in fresh air and breathe out stale air while most of its body remains underwater.

Skin
The whale's skin is smooth and almost hairless. That helps in streamlining, so that the whale cuts through the water easily as it swims. To keep heat inside the body, the whale has a thick insulating layer of fatty tissue called blubber beneath the skin.

Eyes and ears
The eyes can see both above and below the water, but the sense of hearing is more important. The two ear openings are visible only as tiny holes on the body surface.

Flippers
The flippers steer the whale and help in braking. They contain "arm" and "hand" bones and five "fingers", which are present in the forelimbs of most mammals.

Skeleton
The killer whale skeleton is broad and thickset. The skull is very long and thin, with a snout at the front. That shape provides streamlining plus large jaws for grasping prey. The backbone is usually made up of 52 small bones, called vertebrae. The neck vertebrae are fused (joined); that stops the head from wobbling when the whale swims. There are no hind limbs. The tail vertebrae move against one another, like the links in a chain, allowing large swimming movements.

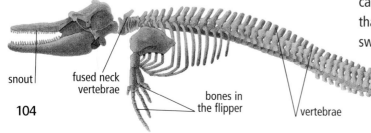

snout

fused neck vertebrae

bones in the flipper

vertebrae

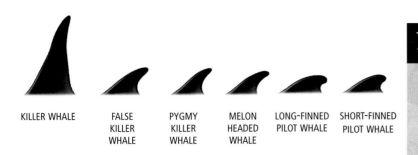

KILLER WHALE | FALSE KILLER WHALE | PYGMY KILLER WHALE | MELON HEADED WHALE | LONG-FINNED PILOT WHALE | SHORT-FINNED PILOT WHALE

Dorsal fins and body sizes

The killer whale's dorsal fin is the largest and most upright of any dolphin or whale. It may be up to 6.5 feet (2 m) tall in males. The killer whale is slightly larger than the pilot whale (below).

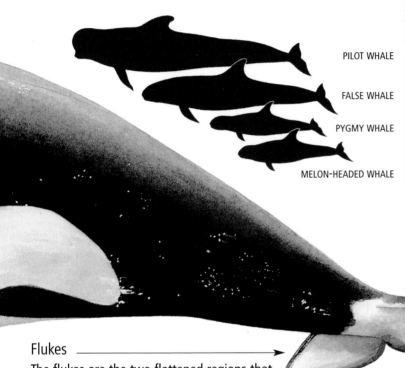

PILOT WHALE

FALSE WHALE

PYGMY WHALE

MELON-HEADED WHALE

Flukes

The flukes are the two flattened regions that make up the tail. They contain muscles and tendons that connect to the backbone. When sets of muscles shorten, they cause the tail to bend. The whale swishes its flukes up and down to drive its body forward.

FACT FILE

The male killer whale, or orca, (above center) can reach up to 32 feet (9.8 m) in length. Long-finned pilot whales may reach just over 26 feet (8 m). At 9 feet (2.7 m) in length, the pygmy killer whale (above left) is the smallest killer whale, along with the melon-headed whale.

Killer whale

GENUS: *Orcinus*
SPECIES: *orca*

SIZE

HEAD–BODY LENGTH: male 21–32 feet (6.5–9.8 m); female 20–28 feet (6–8.5 m)
WEIGHT: male 4–9 tons (3.6–8 metric tons); female 2.5–3.5 tons (2.3–3.2 metric tons)

COLORATION

Easy to recognize, with the back and flanks mostly black except for a white patch behind each eye, a gray saddle behind the dorsal (back) fin, and a white patch on the lower flank behind the dorsal fin. The underside is white; the dorsal fin and flippers are black; and the underside of the flukes are white.

Skull

There are between 20 and 26 cone-shaped teeth in both the upper and lower jaws. They interlock when the jaws close. These teeth grasp and bite but do not chew; prey is swallowed whole or in large chunks.

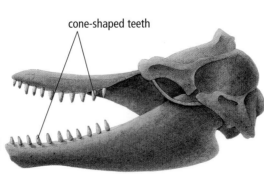

cone-shaped teeth

Whale tooth

The teeth have growth lines, like the rings in a tree trunk. Scientists can count the growth lines to tell the age of a whale.

growth lines

Porpoising and spy-hopping

K iller whales spend most of their time swimming, hunting, and playing. Approximately half of their time is spent traveling from one place to another and hunting for food. Up to one third of their time is spent in playful and social behavior. Sometimes killer whales play with dead or live prey in a form of "cat and

Above: *Killer whales live in strong family groups. Rare among mammals, they are protective toward one another.*

mouse." Social play often involves them in acrobatics and touching and nuzzling other members of the pod. The remaining two to three hours of the day are spent resting and sleeping.

Knowledge about killer whales is based largely on what can be seen when they come to the surface. They rise every few minutes to breathe and sometimes they swim along at or just below the surface,

DID YOU KNOW ?

Diving details

A killer whale's prey lives at shallow depths and so orcas rarely need to dive deeper than 1,640 feet (500 m). When traveling or hunting, a killer whale's typical dive pattern is four or five short dives of less than half a minute each, followed by a long dive of 5 to 10 minutes. After each dive, the whale comes up to breathe, puffing out the air from its lungs in a recognizable blow that looks like a spray of water. The blow contains water droplets and mucus (a slippery secretion) and has a very fishy smell.

arcing out of the water at regular intervals in a movement called porpoising. Occasionally they rise up slowly out of the water, as though standing on their tails, to look around, a behavior called spy-hopping. Sometimes they fling themselves out of the water and crash back in, an action called breaching. Breaching probably serves different purposes at different times. Sometimes it may be a warning to other killer whales. Occasionally killer whales breach to herd fish and other prey into a tight school to make them easier to catch. Sometimes killer whales may breach simply for fun or to remove skin parasites.

Seeing with sound

Sunlight does not reach very far into seawater. If killer whales relied on their sight for hunting, they would not be able to hunt at depths greater than around 500 feet (150 m) or at night. Instead, killer whales rely greatly on sound. Like other toothed whales, killer whales send out a beam of clicks through their forehead and then listen for the echoes. These echoes are channeled through the lower jaw to reach their ears. The echoes provide a great deal of information, such as the size, shape, distance, and movement of any nearby objects, such as prey and other whales. This "seeing-with-sound" method is called echolocation. Toothed whales can even "see" the internal structure of their prey, rather like an X-ray, using echolocation.

AMAZING FACTS

• Killer whales are among the fastest swimming whales of all, reaching speeds of 35 miles per hour (55 km/h). They are able to outswim almost all fish, except billfish such as marlin, sailfish, and swordfish.

Below: *A killer whale pod swims around on the ocean surface. One whale is breaching, leaping completely out of the water to crash back in.*

A lesson in killing

Above: *When cooperating to catch salmon, the killer whales' first tactic is to swim after the fish in a line. The whales then surround the salmon school and snatch up each fish as it tries to escape.*

DID YOU KNOW?

The Bay of Plenty

Several pods of resident killer whales live in the waters around New Zealand in the southern hemisphere. In winter, two or more pods gather in the waters of the Bay of Plenty to feed on the fish and squid that gather there. The Bay of Plenty is situated on the north coast of New Zealand's North Island. It is a wildlife hot spot. Many animals flock here to avoid the icy currents that sweep up from the Southern Ocean in Antarctica—and the killer whales are waiting for them. Sometimes the whales hunt alone; and at other times, the members of a pod cooperate as a team. In yet other cases, different pods of killer whales come together to feed, showing little aggression.

Killer whales are expert hunters, fully justifying their name. A fully grown male killer whale living in cold water needs to eat as much as 220 pounds (100 kg) of food a day to maintain itself and keep warm. That amount of food is equal to four seal pups, or a dozen or so salmon, or 300 to 400 herring.

Working together in a pod, killer whales can outswim or overpower almost any animal in the ocean. By cooperating, the individuals in a pod can round up, tire out, and even stun their prey. Pods often have preferred prey, and the older members of the pod teach the younger ones how to hunt them. They show by example and also teach the youngsters through play. For example, an older killer whale may catch and release a wounded sea lion pup close to a young whale, giving the youngster the chance to make its first kill.

Different pods of killer whales match their hunting technique to the local prey. In the Southern Ocean around Antarctica, for example, some killer whales nudge ice flows to knock sleeping seals or penguins into the water and into the waiting mouths of other pod members.

In Alaska, some pods hunt herring. Killer whales swim around a school of herring, gradually panicking the prey so they bunch up just beneath the sea surface. Then one or two pod members swim into the tightly packed shoal. The whales slap their tails violently, creating underwater shock waves that stun some of the fish. The whales then glide in and pick off the dazed, drifting fish one by one.

Off Patagonia, Argentina, and the Crozet islands of the Indian Ocean, killer whales even leave the water to catch their prey. Sea lions and elephant seals breed on particular beaches, and killer whales are waiting for their pups. Some whales have even learned the risky business of swimming fast into the

PREY

The range of food items on a killer whale's menu is astonishing. They eat almost anything that swims in the sea, including salmon, cod, herring, sea otters, squid, cuttlefish, sharks, walruses, sea turtles, and narwhals. Other prey includes:

PENGUIN (family Spheniscidae)
Killer whales feast on penguins, such as the jackass and king penguin, as well as other seabirds, including gulls, frigate birds, and boobies.

SEAL (families Phocidae and Otariidae)
AND SEA LION (family Otariidae)
Even on land, sea lion pups are not safe because killer whales risk their own lives to beach themselves to snatch the pups from the shoreline.

SPINNER DOLPHIN (family Delphinidae)
Attacking in pods of five or six, killer whales sometimes force dolphins, such as the spinner dolphin, to stay underwater until they drown.

GRAY WHALE (*Eschrichtius robustus*)
Killer whales take even the largest of sea mammals, including the gray whale.

DUGONG (*Dugong dugon*)
AND MANATEE (*Trichechus* species)
Despite measuring up to 15 feet (4.6 m) in length, dugongs and manatees are preyed on by sharks and killer whales.

CARIBOU (*Rangifer tarandus*) **AND MOOSE** (*Alces alces*)
Some deer, such as caribou and moose, are snapped up by killer whales as they swim across bays or rivers.

surf, riding up onto the shore to grab a seal or sea lion pup, and wriggling back into the water without getting stranded.

Left: *A killer whale rides up onto the shore to snatch a sea lion pup. Adults teach this activity to their offspring.*

Inseparable families

SINGLE CALF: In the northern hemisphere killer whales mate between October and December. After 15 to 17 months a single killer whale calf is born. It arrives tail first.

FIRST BREATH: After birth, the mother helps her calf to the surface, where it takes its first breath.

Killer whale

GESTATION: 15–17 months

LENGTH AT BIRTH: 6.6–8 feet (2–2.5 m)

WEIGHT AT BIRTH: 400 pounds (180 kg)

WEANING PERIOD: 18–24 months

LENGTH AT 1 YEAR: 11.5 feet (3.5 m)

SEXUAL MATURITY: Male 14–18 years; female 10–15 years

LENGTH WHEN SEXUALLY MATURE: Male 18–20 feet (5.5–6 m); female 15–16 feet (4.5–5 m)

LIFE SPAN: Male 30–40 years (up to 60); female 50–70 years (up to 90)

A killer whale pod is a family group, usually made up of an elderly mother and her close relatives, including daughters, sons, granddaughters, grandsons, and their close relatives. Mating occurs most often at the end of the summer but it can take place at other times, when pods of killer whales mingle and individuals from different pods court one another. Males usually compete with each other over females, tussling and

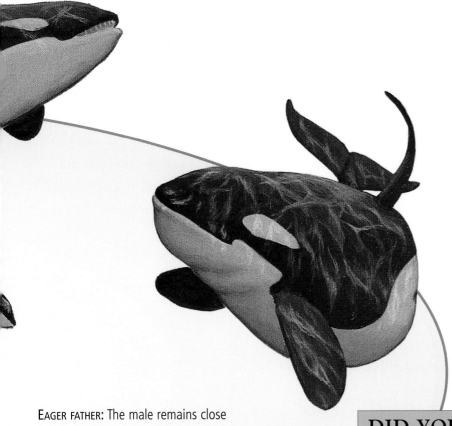

EAGER FATHER: The male remains close to the birthing mother, ready to support her and the new offspring.

The life of a killer whale

DID YOU KNOW?

Killer whale calls

Apart from making clicks for echolocation, killer whales produce high-pitched squeals and screams. An individual whale produces several kinds of calls, which seem to have specific meanings, such as warnings or greetings. Whales recognize the calls of different individuals in their pod just as people recognize the voices of others they know.

rolling around excitedly. The larger, more active males are usually the ones that get to mate with the females.

The baby whale develops inside the mother for at least 15 months before being born through the birth canal. The newborn whale, or calf, can swim but usually needs to be helped to the surface by its mother to take its first breath.

With its mother's help, the calf gradually learns how to swim, dive, and track prey using echolocation (using reflected sound to find objects and figure out distances). For the first year or so, mother and calf swim closely together. When young, the calf is powerless to fend off attacks by sharks, so a mother's protection is vital. The calf suckles its mother's milk for several years but it starts to catch and eat fish and other prey at about 18 months. Killer whale milk is thick and creamy and a rich source of fat and protein for the developing calf.

A change of mind

People's attitudes to killer whales have changed dramatically over the years. Even in the 1950s, for example, sailors thought killer whales might attack them. People also believed that whales competed with fishers for fish and reduced the fishers' catches. In the 1950s, the government of Iceland asked the United States Air Force to bomb and shoot orcas in Icelandic waters to reduce their numbers and to improve the fishing.

Most people now know that they have little to fear from killer whales—and that overfishing by people and not whales is the main cause of the reduction in fish stocks. Changes in attitude have developed because of recent wildlife documentaries and movies, such as 1993's *Free Willy*. Many people have also enjoyed the antics of trained killer whales in oceanariums. Scientists have been studying the 500 or so resident killer whales off the Pacific coast of North America for more than 40 years and they now know a great deal about their behavior.

Hunting

Killer and pilot whales have rarely been hunted in very large numbers, but as late as the 1950s, whalers caught tens of thousands of pilot whales in the northwest Atlantic Ocean. Eventually, so few pilot whales remained that it was not worth the whalers' time and trouble to catch them.

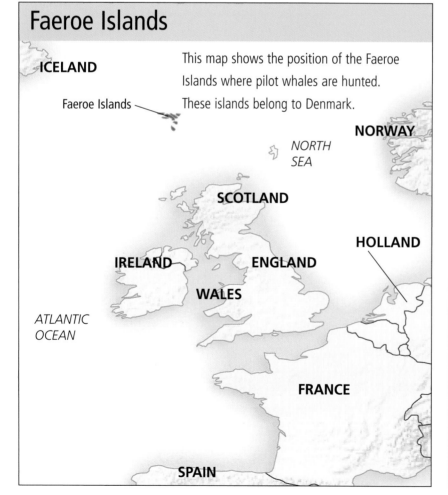

Faeroe Islands

ICELAND

Faeroe Islands

This map shows the position of the Faeroe Islands where pilot whales are hunted. These islands belong to Denmark.

NORWAY

NORTH SEA

SCOTLAND

HOLLAND

IRELAND

ENGLAND

WALES

ATLANTIC OCEAN

FRANCE

SPAIN

At risk

None of the six species of killer whales or pilot whales is greatly threatened in the way that large predators, such as the big cats, are on land. However, the combined effects of fishing, pollution, and disturbance do take a toll on the world population of killer whales.

In the rest of the world, the number of killer whales has been little affected by hunting.

Only a few countries now hunt pilot whales, and then only on a small scale. One such place is the Faeroe Islands, which are situated between the North Atlantic Ocean and the North Sea, approximately halfway between Scotland and Iceland. Each year, following strict regulations, the islanders drive more than 1,000 long-finned pilot whales into bays and kill them to provide local people with meat and blubber.

Until recently, killer whales and pilot whales were captured for display in oceanariums. This activity now attracts unwelcome publicity from conservation and animal welfare groups, which criticize keeping whales in captivity. Even in the best-run oceanariums, for example, whales are separated from the social group that they would normally live with in the wild.

Fishing affects whale populations by removing some of the food supply on which they depend. In addition, some whales become accidentally entangled in fishing nets and then drown.

Pollution problems

Chemical pollution and noise pollution take their toll on killer and other whales. This problem is largely unseen and unrecorded. A major oil spill in 1989, when the tanker *Exxon Valdez* ran aground in Prince William Sound, Alaska, devastated one killer whale pod caught in the pollution. About half of the pod died in the weeks following the spill.

Chemical pollutants that collect in marine animals get passed on through the food chain and eventually build up in killer whales. In Puget Sound, Washington, killer whales contain high levels of industrial chemicals called PCBs, which may reduce their ability to breed properly. This problem has also affected marine mammals such as seals.

Disturbance and noise from boat traffic, including whale-watching vessels, can change the behavior of killer whales. By changing their hunting and breeding behaviors, the success of local pods can be threatened.

CHECK THESE OUT
RELATIVES: • **Dolphins** • Gray whales • Right whales • Rorquals • Sperm whales
PREY: • Gray whales • **Seals, true**

Right: *Killer whales go through their routine at an oceanarium. Scientists have been able to find out a great deal about killer whales in these places.*

MANATEES AND DUGONGS

The West Indian manatee and the dugong are two of four living species of sirenians, or sea cows. Sirenians get their name from the Greek word siren. In Greek mythology, the beauty and haunting songs of mermaids called sirens attracted sailors to their doom.

Below: *A manatee calf feeds from its mother. A calf stays with the mother for one to two years. Like elephants, the manatee's milk glands are positioned near the female's armpits.*

Sirens of the Sea

- **COMMON NAME:** West Indian manatee
- **SCIENTIFIC NAME:** *Trichechus manatus*
- **CLOSELY RELATED SPECIES:** West African manatee (*Trichechus senegalensis*), Amazonian manatee (*Trichechus inunguis*), and dugong (*Dugong dugon*)
- **HABITAT:** Tropical, subtropical, or warm temperate coastal waters, particularly where there is abundant plant growth in or on the water
- **RANGE:** Coastal waters and nearby freshwater of the Atlantic Ocean and Caribbean Sea, from Rhode Island in the north to the easternmost tip of Brazil in the south
- **APPEARANCE:** Low-positioned mouth, small sunken eyes, large rounded flippers, no visible ears; rough gray skin with scattered short hairs; skin often discolored by growths of algae.

It is hard to believe that sailors would mistake a manatee for a mermaid—an imaginary creature that is half woman and half fish. However, when female manatees suckle their young, they sometimes lie on their back and their two milk glands—one in each armpit—might, by a stretch of the imagination, be mistaken for the breasts of a woman.

There are four living species of sirenians: three species of manatees and one species of dugong. A fifth, much larger species, called Steller's sea cow, was discovered by sailors in the subarctic waters of the Bering Sea, between Alaska and Siberia, in 1741. In these chilly waters, the flesh of this slow-moving giant was described by sailors "as good as the best joints of beef." They hunted the animal to extinction within 30 years of its discovery.

Above: A dugong cruises slowly across the seabed, searching for sea grass to graze on. Dugongs are sometimes called sea pigs because they dig up sea grass with their snouts.

RELATIVES

The West Indian manatee (left) is one of four living species of sirenians, or sea cows, members of the order Sirenia. Sirenians are classified within the superorder Paenungulata, or subungulates, which also includes aardvarks, elephants, and hyraxes.

AARDVARK (*Orycteropus afer*)
Inhabiting the grasslands, woodlands, and forests of Africa south of the Sahara desert, aardvarks are solitary and nocturnal. They have a long snout and pinkish gray skin.

AFRICAN ELEPHANT (*Loxodonta africana*)
ASIATIC ELEPHANT (*Elephas maximus*)
These large, plant-eating mammals have large ears, pillarlike legs, and a long trunk. African elephants and male Asiatic elephants have two tusks. Male African elephants are the largest and heaviest land animals. Elephants live in groups called herds in the grasslands and woodlands of Africa and Asia.

DUGONG (*Dugong dugon*)
Slightly smaller than the West Indian and West African manatees, the dugong is the only sirenian that lives in the Indian and Pacific Oceans. Its tail has flukes, like those of a whale, and its mouth and snout are strongly downturned for bottom-feeding.

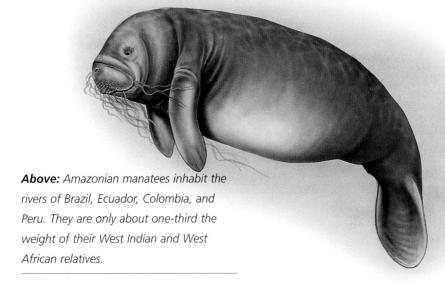

Above: *Amazonian manatees inhabit the rivers of Brazil, Ecuador, Colombia, and Peru. They are only about one-third the weight of their West Indian and West African relatives.*

Blubbery body

Sirenians are rather grizzled creatures, looking something like a cross between a walrus and a small whale. The blunt rounded head merges with the blubbery body, without an obvious neck. Similar to whales, sirenians do not have hind limbs and their tail is flattened horizontally. The animal moves its tail up and down to propel itself forward. Also, like whales, sirenians have flippers; unlike whales, they use them not just for steering and braking, but for sculling through the water at slow speed or "walking" along a shallow seabed or riverbed.

Sirenians are unaggressive creatures that swim slowly through warm coastal waters and nearby freshwaters, feeding on seaweeds, sea grasses, and freshwater plants. In their feeding habits they are quite unlike the other two groups of marine mammals, cetaceans (whales, dolphins, and porpoises) and pinnipeds (seals, sea lions, and walruses), which are all meat eaters. Sirenians are vegetarians but they will take animal prey on rare occasions, when grubbing for clams or taking fish from fisher's nets.

slightly smaller, at up to 13 feet (4 m) long and 2,000 pounds (900 kg). The Amazonian manatee is smaller still, at about 9 feet (2.7 m) and 1,100 pounds (500 kg).

Most scientists recognize two subspecies of West Indian manatees: the Florida manatee lives north of the Antillean manatee. The two species can be distinguished physically only by small differences in the bones of the skull.

Left: *This dugong hovers upright in the water. Dugongs inhabit the oceans from eastern Africa to Vanuatu, an island off the eastern coast of Australia.*

Shape and size

The three species of manatees have paddlelike tails, similar in shape to those of beavers, while the tail of a dugong is extended horizontally, like the flukes of a whale. The dugong's tail is also indented to form a shallow "V" shape.

West Indian and West African manatees can reach up to 14 feet (4.3 m) long and weigh as much as 3,500 pounds (1,590 kg). The dugong is

DID YOU KNOW?

Ancestors

Sirenians evolved from land-living mammals within the last 60 million years. The closest living relatives of sirenians are elephants, with which they share many features. For example, the texture and color of sirenians' sparsely haired skin is similar to that of young elephants. The skull and lower jaw of manatees are remarkably similar to those of elephants, and they have a similar tooth-replacement mechanism: old, worn teeth at the front are replaced by new teeth growing forward from the back. Until about 100,000 years ago, sirenian species were much more varied and widespread than they are now. A combination of cooling climate and hunting by people has reduced the variety of sirenian species and their geographic ranges.

ANATOMY: Manatee

DUGONG

Nostrils
The nostrils are near the tip of the snout.
The manatee breathes with just a small part
of its head visible above the water.

Snout
The snout is deeply
cleft (grooved) to
better grasp plants.

Teeth
The manatee's teeth are
replaced by new teeth growing
forward from the back as old,
worn teeth drop out at the front.

MANATEE TAIL   DUGONG TAIL

Tail
The tail of a manatee is paddle shaped, like that of a beaver,
while the dugong's tail is fluke shaped, like that of a whale.

Flippers
Flippers are short but flexible.
They push food up to the mouth
and help the animal push itself
along the seabed or riverbed.
West Indian and West African
manatees have fingernails.

Skeletons
Manatees and dugongs have large lungs
that, together with the gases produced
in their gut, tend to help them float.
To counter this, manatees have heavy
bones that make them sink.

MANATEE

large, barrel
chest

five fingers
in each flipper

DUGONG

AMAZONIAN
MANATEE

WEST INDIAN
MANATEE

AFRICAN
MANATEE

Manatee and dugong snouts
The shape of the snout and the position of the mouth are related to the area in the water where a sirenian feeds. The waters where Amazonian and West African manatees graze are usually too murky for plants to grow underwater. Therefore , these manatees feed on floating plants and their snouts are less downturned compared with other sirenians. The dugong feeds mostly on the seabed and its mouth is positioned low under the head. The West Indian manatee, which has a more varied diet and feeds at the surface, in midwater, or on the seabed or riverbed, has a snout shape midway between that of other manatees and the dugong.

Skin
The skin is wrinkled, tough, and up to 2 inches (5 cm) thick. In West Indian manatees, the skin is often scarred by injuries from boat propellers.

Tail
The tail is flattened horizontally into a broad paddle. The manatee swishes its tail up and down to propel itself forward.

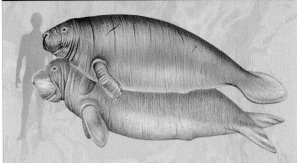
Skulls and jaws
West Indian manatees have 8 to 14 molars (grinding teeth) at the back of each jaw. As the front teeth are worn down by chewing, new teeth move forward from the back to replace them.

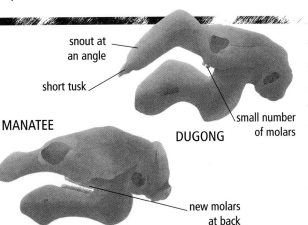

snout at an angle

short tusk

MANATEE

small number of molars

DUGONG

new molars at back

The dugong has only four to six molars at the back of each jaw. The male has two incisor teeth that grow forward as short tusks. Males use these teeth against each other in mock fights over females.

Warm-water migrants

Manatees and dugongs do not like the cold. The heat-trapping layer of blubber beneath their skin is thinner than that of whales. In addition, their vegetarian diet is low in energy and so does not provide much fuel for heating the body. All sirenian species need to stay in tropical, subtropical, or warm temperate waters to avoid chilling. Those sirenians that live at the cool extremes of their range migrate (travel) to warmer water in winter. Some West Indian manatees, for example, move in winter to rivers fed by hot springs or by warm water pumped from power stations.

Plenty of food

Apart from staying warm enough, manatees and dugongs live where there is plenty of plant food. The two largest species of manatees, the West Indian manatee and the West African manatee, are at home both in saltwater and freshwater, although they need to drink freshwater regularly.

The Amazonian manatee spends its entire life in freshwater rivers, while the dugong lives in the sea. The dugong does not need to drink freshwater but manages to get the water it needs from the plants it eats.

Manatees and dugongs prefer sheltered waters, where waves, tides, and currents are gentle. That encourages the lush growth of underwater or floating plants, which these animals eat. Sirenians prefer to live in shallow water or in water that is full of obstructions, such as mangrove tree roots. In these habitats, manatees and dugongs are safest because dangerous sharks and predatory whales have difficulty reaching them.

Easy targets

Being such slow-moving animals that must regularly come to the surface to breathe, sirenians have always been easy targets for people.

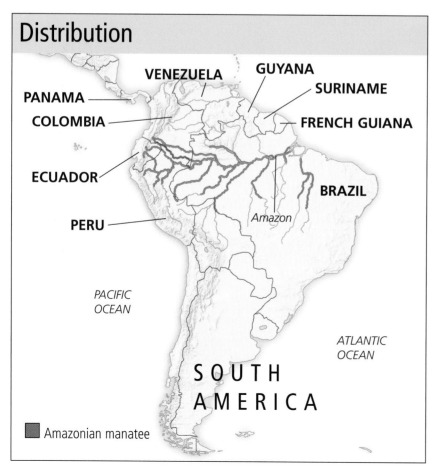

Distribution

PANAMA

VENEZUELA

GUYANA

SURINAME

COLOMBIA

FRENCH GUIANA

ECUADOR

BRAZIL

PERU

Amazon

PACIFIC OCEAN

ATLANTIC OCEAN

SOUTH AMERICA

■ Amazonian manatee

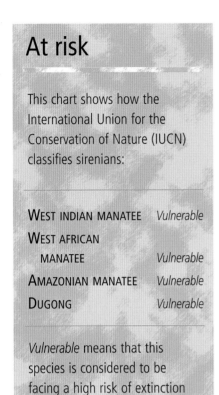

At risk

This chart shows how the International Union for the Conservation of Nature (IUCN) classifies sirenians:

WEST INDIAN MANATEE	*Vulnerable*
WEST AFRICAN MANATEE	*Vulnerable*
AMAZONIAN MANATEE	*Vulnerable*
DUGONG	*Vulnerable*

Vulnerable means that this species is considered to be facing a high risk of extinction in the wild.

By the nineteenth century, the populations of all four remaining species had been greatly reduced by hunting. Since then, sirenians have had to cope with a whole new set of problems. For example, boats powered by propellers cruise back and forth across the water, and manatees and dugongs are slow to get out of the way. In Florida alone, despite regulations to keep boat speeds down, dozens of manatees are struck by powered craft each year and are killed or injured.

Sirenians are also in danger of being accidentally caught and drowned in fishing nets. In addition, the places where they live are being altered or destroyed as developers build new towns and industries close to coastal waters and estuaries (mouths of rivers). Sea grass, on which dugongs and coastal manatees feed, are threatened by dredging (deepening the waterways), propeller damage, silting (filling up with sandlike material), and pollution. Manatees and dugongs breed slowly, producing only a few young in a lifetime. As a result, they cannot replace their numbers quickly.

Right: *A West Indian manatee cruises in warm, shallow waters. These animals were once common and widespread in the coastal and river waters of the southeastern United States, Central America, and northern South America.*

A quiet life

On a typical summer's day, a manatee spends about eight hours eating underwater vegetation and four to five hours resting in a drowsy state. Whether active or inactive, manatees float to the surface every few minutes to breathe. Some scientists figured out that manatees spend up to 12 hours a day relaxing and playing. They form loose groups in which they playfully chase each other, occasionally nuzzling snout to snout or clasping their flippers around each other.

Although manatees have small eyes, they can see quite well underwater, even in poor light. Hearing and touch are also important. Using its larynx, or voice box, a manatee can produce a wide range of sounds. They include high-pitched squeaks, squeals, and whistles to low-pitched rumbles that can be felt more than heard. Alarm calls cause manatees to gather together for safety in numbers or rush to escape. Female manatees probably give off low-frequency sounds to attract males when they are ready to breed.

DID YOU KNOW?

Short, shallow divers

Sirenians dive with their lungs full of air, and as the dive proceeds they gradually use up the oxygen contained in the air. Their dives are neither long nor deep, unlike supreme deep divers such as whales and seals. Manatees tend to dive for up to 20 minutes and rarely to depths greater than 60 feet (18 m). Dugong dives tend to last 10 minutes or less.

Right: A manatee rubs against underwater rocks to leave its scent. These scents inform the other manatees about the individual's age and sex and whether it is ready to mate.

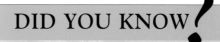

DID YOU KNOW?

Rubbing post

Some manatees regularly rub themselves against favorite underwater features, such as rocks and logs. When they do so, they leave a scent marking that advertises their presence. The scent may include information such as the individual animal's age, sex, and readiness to mate, which other manatees can detect.

The scattering of 1– to 2–inch (2.5–5 cm) long hairs across the body surface acts as touch detectors. The hairs bend in response to water movements, such as those produced by manatees or other creatures swimming close by.

Left: *Two manatees nuzzle snout to snout. For manatees, this "kissing" is a form of greeting. It also helps the animals recognize one another.*

AMAZING FACTS

• Manatee and dugong nostrils close automatically when the animal dives underwater.

• When the animal rises to take a breath, it can empty and fill its lungs within five seconds.

• When it takes a breath, a manatee renews about 90 percent of the air in its lungs. A human renews only about 15 percent of the air in his or her lungs when taking a breath.

Hearty appetites

The common name for sirenians is sea cows. This description is fitting because it compares manatees and dugongs with the slow, vegetation-chewing cattle that live on land.

The West Indian manatee is the most varied feeder among sirenians. In freshwater it eats floating plants, such as water hyacinth, and rooted underwater plants, such as wild celery and water achillea.

It even browses leaves on overhanging branches or hauls itself partly out of the water to get at tasty bankside vegetation. In coastal waters, West Indian manatees eat seaweeds and seagrass.

Amazonian and West African manatees tend to live in murky waters where rooted underwater plants cannot grow. Therefore, they eat floating plants or plants that hang over or grow alongside the water.

Flippers, tongues, and teeth

All three manatee species use their flippers to direct food to the mouth. They grasp their plant food in the cleft (groove) between the two halves of the upper lip, which work together like tweezers to move the food into the mouth. The tongue steers the food to the back of the mouth where large, grinding molar teeth gradually reduce the food into a pulp before swallowing.

Left: Dugongs graze on sea grass. Tough pads on the upper and lower jaws allow them to chew their tough food. They have only a few peglke molars at the back of the jaw.

Vegetation is tough and fibrous, and a manatee's teeth get worn down in the process of chewing. The molars grow forward at the rate of about 0.04 inch (1 mm) every month. By the time worn-out teeth at the front of the mouth have dropped out, new teeth have grown forward at the back to replace them.

Going without

Manatees eat a huge amount of food each day. A large West Indian manatee, for example, eats around 200 pounds (90 kg) a day. Despite their hearty appetites when food is available, manatees can go without food when there is not enough during the winter or at times of drought. The West Indian manatee may go without food for a week or more in winter, while the Amazonian manatee may go without food for up to six months during the dry season. When fasting, manatees move around less to save energy and use the energy stores in their blubber.

Dugong diets

Dugongs favor the energy-rich roots of sea grass and dig them up with their snout. They grasp the newly uprooted plant in

PREDATORS

Sirenians have few predators but have been known to be attacked by killer whales and sharks.

KILLER WHALE (*Orcinus orca*)
The largest member of the dolphin family, the killer whale swims and hunts in all oceans. Orcas eat almost any medium to large-sized prey they can overpower.

BULL SHARK (*Carcharhinus leucas*)
Like manatees, the bull shark is able to swim between freshwater and saltwater, making it the most dangerous shark to sirenians.

NEIGHBORS

The mangrove swamps of the Florida Everglades are home to the Florida manatee. Many other animals live in Florida's subtropical habitats, including:

LEMON SHARK (*Negaprion brevirostris*)
Lemon sharks cruise Florida's shallow coastal waters hunting for fish.

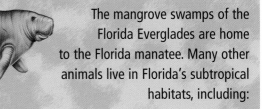

AMERICAN ALLIGATOR (*Alligator mississippiensis*)
This ferocious predator lives in the warm swamps of the southeastern United States.

SNAPPING TURTLE (family Chelydridae)
With its hugely powerful jaws, a snapping turtle is capable of killing baby alligators.

their overhanging and strongly cleft upper lips and shake the plants to remove mud or grains of sand. At the front of the mouth, ridged pads, rather than teeth, start the chewing process. At the back of the mouth there are up to six premolar and six molar teeth in both the upper and lower jaws. These teeth grind the plant food to a soft pulp before swallowing.

When most dugong teeth wear or fall out, they are not replaced. However, the back pair of molar teeth in each jaw grow throughout life. Dugongs graze so well that they leave cleared tracks through sea grass beds where they have fed.

Strong mother-calf bond

Manatees do not tend to form close-knit family and friendship groups as are common among whales and dolphins. When sirenians gather in large groups, it is usually because they have found good feeding grounds, favorable conditions in their surroundings, or as protection against predators. They also gather to breed. The strongest social ties are between the mother and calf.

Although West Indian manatees may mate at any time of the year, most favor the summer months when food is abundant. The single calf is born about 13 months later, when vegetation is plentiful as food for the nursing mother. When a female manatee (cow) is ready to breed, she is followed by up to a dozen or more males. They jostle each other and pester the cow until one or more of the largest and most forceful males succeeds in mating with her. The males then go off to find other females and play no further role in the lives of the mother and her calf.

AMONG SIRENIANS, THE STRONGEST SOCIAL TIES ARE BETWEEN MOTHER AND CALF.

The bond between mother and calf is strong. They regularly nuzzle snout to snout, which looks like kissing, and the calf calls to its mother with a variety of calls to which she responds.

The mother's milk is thick and creamy. She does not store it, so the calf has to feed little and often.

Breeding behavior in dugongs is similar to that of manatees, but dugongs mature more slowly and produce fewer offspring in a lifetime. Also, when male dugongs compete with each other for access to females, they do so by claiming territories, which they firmly defend. A male dugong uses its short tusks to fend off any other male that enters its territory, and most adult males bear scars from such battles.

West Indian manatee

GESTATION: 12–14 months
NUMBER OF YOUNG: 1
LENGTH AT BIRTH: 31–63 inches (79–160 cm)
WEIGHT AT BIRTH: 66 pounds (30 kg)
WEANING PERIOD: About 18 months
SEXUAL MATURITY: 6–8 years
LIFE SPAN: Up to 60–70 years

CHECK THESE OUT
RELATIVES: • Elephants   PREDATORS: • **Killer whales**

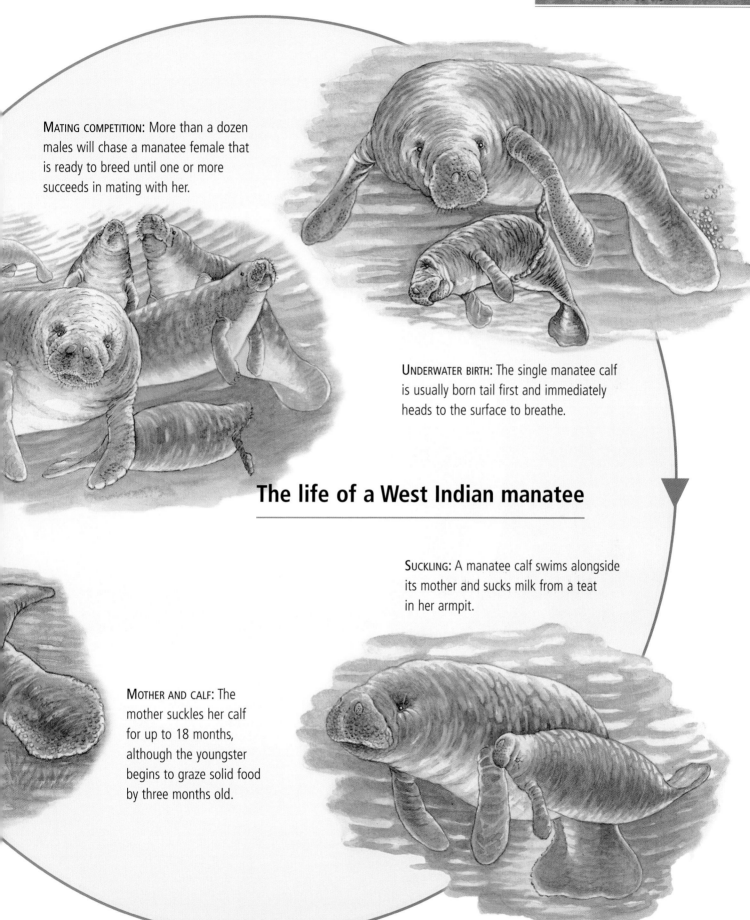

MATING COMPETITION: More than a dozen males will chase a manatee female that is ready to breed until one or more succeeds in mating with her.

UNDERWATER BIRTH: The single manatee calf is usually born tail first and immediately heads to the surface to breathe.

The life of a West Indian manatee

SUCKLING: A manatee calf swims alongside its mother and sucks milk from a teat in her armpit.

MOTHER AND CALF: The mother suckles her calf for up to 18 months, although the youngster begins to graze solid food by three months old.

PANDAS

Pandas are among the world's best-loved animals, but they are also among the most endangered. People are now making great efforts to protect these bears and the fragile forest environment they need to survive.

Below: *A giant panda sits aloft in a tree. Each adult panda has a well-defined home range in bamboo forests in Sichuan, Shaanxi, and Gansu provinces of central and western China.*

Bamboo Forest Stars

G iant pandas are among the most easily recognized animals on Earth. Their large heads and striking black and white fur makes these bears stand out from other mammals. Giant pandas have also become well known as one of the rarest mammals on Earth.

In the 1960s, the panda was chosen as the logo for the World Wildlife Fund—the world's largest conservation charity, now known simply as WWF.

The panda became a symbol for all endangered animal species. It is now protected in the forests of China.

As well as their cuddly appearance, other things make giant pandas appealing to people, perhaps because they are humanlike. For example,

Above: With its striped face mask and pointed ears, the red panda looks very similar to its close relative, the raccoon. Red pandas are vegetarian; they eat bamboo, fruit, roots, lichen, and acorns.

KEY FACTS

- **COMMON NAME:** Giant panda
- **SCIENTIFIC NAME:** *Ailuropoda melanoleuca*
- **FAMILY:** Ursidae
- **HABITAT:** Bamboo forests
- **RANGE:** China
- **APPEARANCE:** Giant pandas are black and white bears with a rounded head. The eyes are ringed by dark patches. Giant pandas have a sixth finger made from a piece of wrist bone.

- **COMMON NAME:** Red panda
- **SCIENTIFIC NAME:** *Ailurus fulgens*
- **FAMILY:** Ailuridae
- **HABITAT:** Bamboo forests
- **RANGE:** China
- **APPEARANCE:** Red pandas have a rounded head and thick red hair. The dark bands across the cheeks and the striped bushy tail make the animal look similar to a raccoon.

pandas sit with their legs out in front of them like people and they hold their food in their paws.

Hide or seek

The black patches around a panda's eyes are very distinctive. It is most likely that a panda's patterned coat allows individuals to find each other. Pandas spend a lot of their lives alone in dense bamboo. They prefer to avoid each other but need to come together to breed. They do not have many predators so there is no need to stay hidden. Instead, their bright white coat makes it easier for the bears to see each other through the forest. Once a panda knows where others are, it can choose to stay on its own or go looking for a mate.

Black and white, and red all over

Not all pandas are black and white. The red panda is another Chinese mammal that also lives in bamboo forests. It is much smaller than the giant panda. Local people call it the cat bear, and it is about the same size as a large house cat.

As well as the difference in size, red pandas and giant pandas look different in many other ways. For example, apart from creamy patches on the face and forehead, red pandas have a coat of red hair. However, the two species share some features. Their skull and teeth are similar, and both pandas hold their bamboo food in their forepaws. The giant panda does this with a fingerlike projection. The bear also uses this projection to strip the bamboo. The red panda has a similar bulge on its forepaw, but it is not as large as a giant panda's.

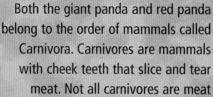

RELATIVES

Both the giant panda and red panda belong to the order of mammals called Carnivora. Carnivores are mammals with cheek teeth that slice and tear meat. Not all carnivores are meat eaters, however. The giant panda is a member of the bear family, Ursidae. Red pandas are sometimes listed in the Procyonidae family, which includes raccoons. However, biologists increasingly think the red panda belongs in a family of its own called Ailuridae. Panda relatives include:

BLACK BEAR (family Ursidae)
There are two species of black bears. The American black bear is the larger of the two. It lives in forests across North America. The Asiatic black bear is sometimes called the moon bear.

BROWN BEAR (Ursus arctos)
Brown bears live across the northern hemisphere. The largest brown bears live in Alaska. The smallest brown bears are found in the Middle East.

POLAR BEAR (Ursus maritimus)
These bears are the largest predators on land, along with Alaskan brown bears. Polar bears hunt on the ice around the Arctic Ocean.

SLOTH BEAR (Melursus ursinus)
Sloth bears are very hairy. They live in southern Asia, where they feed on insects.

RACCOON (Procyon species)
Raccoons are small carnivores that belong to the Procyonidae family. This family also includes kinkajous, ringtails, and coatis.

Right: A red panda has distinctive stripes on its face and its long, bushy tail. It is named for its chestnut-red fur. Red pandas are small; they are only about 8 inches (20 cm) high at the shoulder and weigh about 11 pounds (5 kg).

DID YOU KNOW**?**

What is the relationship?

Although they are both called pandas, biologists took a long time to figure out how giant pandas and red pandas are related. The species had similar features but they also shared other features with different members of the order Carnivora. That made scientists unsure how pandas were linked to other mammals. For example, was the giant panda a very large relative of raccoons, or was the red panda a very small type of bear?

Fossils have been found of a tiny version of the giant panda that lived about 2 million years ago. Giant pandas are thought to have evolved about 1 million years ago, when they lived across what is now China. Red pandas are descended from a raccoonlike animal that lived about 25 million years ago.

Biologists studied the genes of both pandas and discovered that giant pandas are related to bears. Red pandas are more closely related to raccoons than they are to giant pandas. Raccoons and red pandas must have evolved to look similar because they live in similar habitats and eat the same food.

Right: A giant panda strips the leaves off a bamboo shoot and eats them. Giant pandas have a fingerlike projection on each forepaw, which it uses to peel off the bamboo leaves. Over millions of years, these fingers evolved from the panda's wrist bones.

ANATOMY: Giant panda

PANDA

BROWN BEAR

Eyes

The giant panda has excellent vision and can see well at night. Unlike other bears, a panda's pupils form narrow slits when the light is very bright, like those of a cat. The eyes of other bears have rounded pupils.

Paws and claws

The giant panda has five toes on each paw. Each toe has a claw. Each forepaw also has a lump, or fingerlike projection, that pokes out like a thumb. Giant pandas use this projection to hold and strip bamboo. Red pandas have more fur on their paws than giant pandas. There is also a lump on the red panda's forepaw but it is not as large or as movable as the giant panda's.

RED PANDA

FOREPAW

HIND PAW

furry undersides

lump

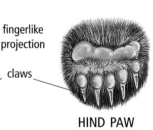

GIANT PANDA

FOREPAW

fingerlike projection

claws

HIND PAW

Fingerlike projection

Giant pandas have a fingerlike projection made from a piece of wrist bone. It is sometimes called a false thumb and can move across the paw like a human thumb.

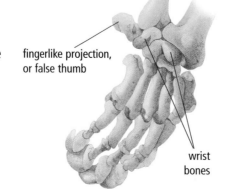

fingerlike projection, or false thumb

wrist bones

Skeleton

A giant panda's skeleton looks similar to those of other bears. However, it has a very large skull. The big head is covered in huge jaw muscles that are used to crush bamboo stalks.

Thick fur
The giant panda's hairs are coated with oil. That keeps the bears waterproof in the rainy bamboo forests.

Hind legs
Like other bears, giant pandas can stand on their hind legs but they cannot walk upright.

Male giant pandas are about 10 percent larger than the females. The giant panda (above right) is much larger than the red panda (above left). It is at least 35 inches (90 cm) high and weighs 275 pounds (125 kg). The red panda is only 8 inches (20 cm) high and weighs about 11 pounds (5 kg).

Giant panda

GENUS: *Ailuropoda*
SPECIES: *melanoleuca*

SIZE
LENGTH: 5–5.5 feet (1.5–1.7 m)
SHOULDER HEIGHT: 30–40 inches (80–100 cm)
TAIL LENGTH: 10 inches (25 cm)
WEIGHT: 175–275 pounds (80–125 kg)

COLORATION
Most of the body and head is white or pale cream. The legs are black, with a black band running over the shoulders. The ears are black and there is a black patch around each eye.

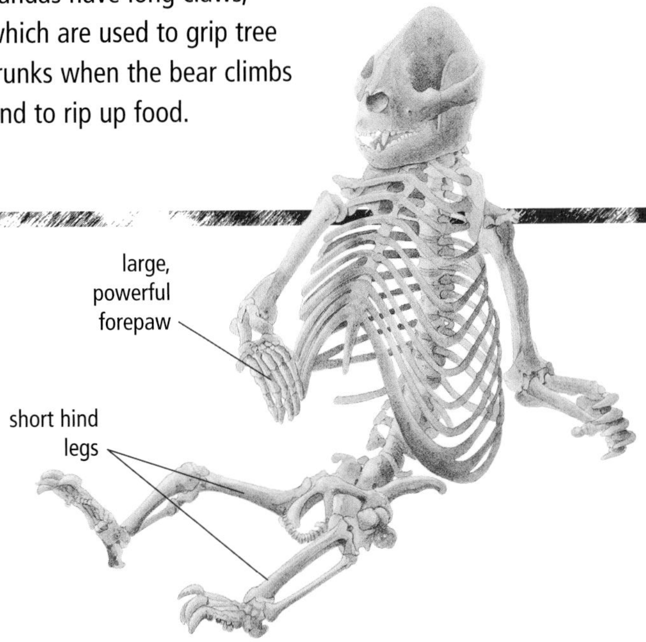

Claws
Pandas have long claws, which are used to grip tree trunks when the bear climbs and to rip up food.

large, powerful forepaw

short hind legs

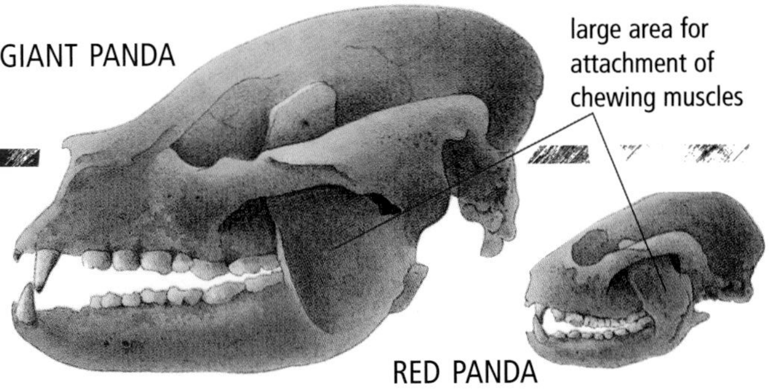

GIANT PANDA

large area for attachment of chewing muscles

RED PANDA

Teeth and skulls
Both species of panda have teeth suited for eating tough bamboo. The molars are wide and flat for crushing and grinding. Strong muscles attach to the heavy skull for chewing.

133

Bamboo lifeline

The giant panda lives only in China. It inhabits damp bamboo forests that grow on the mountains of southern China. The red panda also lives mainly in China, in bamboo forests that grow on the edge of the Tibetan Plateau. Both types of pandas are specialists: they eat mainly bamboo and could not survive outside a bamboo forest.

About 12,000 years ago, there were bamboo forests and pandas right across eastern Asia. That was during the last ice age, when most of the northern hemisphere was covered in ice. However, Sichuan, the area of southern China where pandas now live, was free of ice and protected by mountains. Bamboo forests also covered most of this ice-free land.

All change for Sichuan

The ice began to melt around 12,000 years ago. Everywhere became warmer and drier, and the bamboo forests began to be replaced with trees. The only place that was wet and cold enough for bamboo forests to grow was on the sides of the mountains in Sichuan. These forests were the only places where pandas could also survive. Now the pandas' forests grow at altitudes from 6,500 to 9,800 feet (2,000–3,000 m).

Sichuan is about the size of Kansas and is home to more than 100 million people. Living in such a crowded place, the people of Sichuan have been forced to turn many of the mountain slopes into farms. Only small areas of bamboo forest now remain. With so little of their forest habitat left, only around 1,000 giant pandas survive in the wild. Many of them live in protected reserves. However, the reserves often contain small patches of

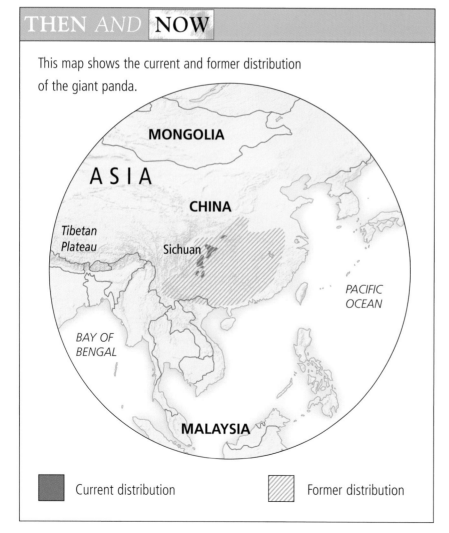

THEN AND NOW

This map shows the current and former distribution of the giant panda.

MONGOLIA

ASIA

CHINA

Tibetan Plateau

Sichuan

PACIFIC OCEAN

BAY OF BENGAL

MALAYSIA

Current distribution

Former distribution

bamboo forest that are unconnected. Conservationists are growing corridors of bamboo to connect these patches. They hope these corridors will allow pandas to spread out, meet mates, and increase their numbers.

Below: *An adult giant panda relaxes in its forest home. Giant pandas live only in the damp bamboo forests that grow on the mountains of southern China in Sichuan province.*

DID YOU KNOW?

First release into the wild

In April 2006, a giant panda bred in captivity was set free into the wild for the first time ever. The Wolong Giant Panda Research Center in Sichuan province released the five-year-old male named Xiang Xiang. He had been born in the research center in 2001 and his keepers had taught him the skills that would prepare the bear for survival in the wild.

There are currently about 180 pandas living in captivity, but fewer than 10 pandas have been born outside China. Pandas are known for being difficult to breed in captivity, but zoos have had more success in China. In the early 2000s, Chinese biologists began using artificial insemination: instead of waiting for a male and female to mate, both pandas are put to sleep and sperm is taken from the male and put into the female at just the right time for her to get pregnant. This technique produces about 20 panda cubs every year.

At risk

This chart shows how the International Union for the Conservation of Nature (IUCN) classifies pandas:

GIANT PANDA	*Endangered*
RED PANDA	*Endangered*

Endangered means that this species faces a very high risk of extinction in the wild if nothing is done.

The simple life

Above: *A dominant (high-ranking) male panda (left) shows his senior status by staring down at his rival.*

Giant pandas live a very simple life. They do little but eat and sleep. Each day pandas eat for 16 hours and sleep for 8. Bamboo is so low in nutrients that pandas must eat almost constantly to stay alive. Pandas often take two naps of four hours. They do not rest in a den: their oiled fur keeps them dry while they sleep in the open.

Territorial maneuvers

Each panda has its own territory. The bear does not spend much time defending this area because it is so busy eating.

Pandas can see and hear each other as they move around their territories and they keep out of each other's way. There is no reason to take over another panda's territory. One area is just as good as another. Bamboo is all a panda needs and it grows everywhere.

A male panda's territory overlaps those of several females. He comes into contact with these females once a year during the breeding season. If rival males meet, they avoid a fight. Their black-and-white faces are easy to see, and pandas

DID YOU KNOW?

Sob story

A story about how pandas got their black-and-white fur is told in a Chinese legend. Pandas were once white all over and were very friendly. One day a panda was playing with a shepherdess. When a leopard attacked them, the girl was killed protecting the panda. At the funeral, all the pandas followed the local custom and covered their arms with ashes. The pandas wiped away their tears and covered their ears to block out the sounds of their crying. The ash left dark marks on their fur. The pandas also hugged to comfort each other, leaving a dark band on their shoulders. From that day on, according to the story, all panda fur has had black markings in the same places.

use them to communicate. The bears stare at each other until the weaker panda turns away. If the two animals are evenly matched, they nod their heads up and down. They then swat each other with their forepaws until one bear backs down.

Pandas mark their territories using glands under their tail. Pandas leave scent marks by rubbing their rears on patches of open ground. Sometimes they mark tree trunks by performing a handstand, so their rear end reaches high up the trunk.

Right: Female giant pandas spend most of their time in a small core area within their own home range. In a typical month, each female panda will visit only around 10 percent of her entire range.

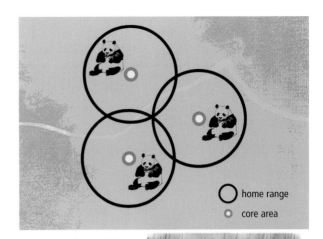

home range
core area

Above: Scent marking is the panda's way of leaving messages. Beneath its short tail is a patch of skin richly supplied with scent glands. The patch is usually rubbed against the ground.

Right: Sometimes, a giant panda performs a backward handstand up a tree to leave its mark. This allows the panda to rub its scent glands high above the ground.

Vegetarian carnivores

Left: A red panda takes a rest in a tree. Red pandas spend much of their time in the trees of the Sichuan forests, where they save their energy by sleeping.

Both giant pandas and red pandas belong to the mammal group called Carnivora. Most other carnivores are fierce meat-eating hunters, such as lions, polar bears, and wolverines. The word *carnivore* means "meat eater" in Latin. Yet neither giant pandas nor red pandas eat much meat at all. Giant pandas eat almost nothing but bamboo. A tiny part of their diet consists of the insects that are on the bamboo as it goes into the panda's mouth. Red pandas also eat a lot of bamboo but they have a more varied diet. They also eat fruit and raid birds' nests for chicks and eggs.

Giant pandas eat by grabbing the tall bamboo stems between their thumb and claws. They push the stem into the side of the mouth. The woody bamboo is crushed by the panda's immense jaws and teeth and is then swallowed.

Just passing through

A panda's gut cannot get much of the nutrients from its food. Bamboo does not have many nutrients in it, anyway, which is why pandas have to spend so much time eating. A stomachful of bamboo is digested for just five hours before passing out as droppings. That

Below: A red panda uses its small false thumb to grasp bamboo leaves while standing up on its hind legs.

is why giant pandas sleep for only four hours at a time. If they slept for any longer, they would begin to starve.

Giant pandas eat all parts of many bamboo plants. Red pandas eat just the leaves of one species of bamboo—arrow bamboo. Red pandas use their smaller thumbs to grab bamboo stems as they bite off the leaves.

Bamboo plants do not flower every year. Instead, they produce flowers every few decades. After a forest of bamboo flowers, all the plants die to make way for the new seedlings. That has led to pandas starving. In 1974, for example, the bamboo at the Wanglang panda reserve flowered and died. All but 20 of the 200 pandas starved to death.

Right: *A giant panda sits down to eat its bamboo meal. Pandas usually sit or lie down to eat, which helps save precious energy.*

AMAZING FACTS

- Bamboo is a large type of grass.
- Bamboo can grow 4 feet (1.3 m) in just one day. That makes it the fastest-growing land plant in the world.
- A male giant panda may eat up to 90 pounds (40 kg) of bamboo in one day. It needs this huge amount to survive.
- Giant pandas produce about 20 droppings every day.

PREY

Pandas were once preyed on by several large hunters, such as leopards and tigers. However, while pandas have become rarer and more endangered, so have their predators. Pandas now have only a few natural enemies, including:

DHOLE (*Cuon alpinus*)
This rare species is also called the Asian hunting dog. It always lives in packs and is a fierce killer.

SNOW LEOPARD (*Uncia uncia*)
This is one of the smallest of the big cats. Like the panda, it now lives only on the mountains of East Asia and is extremely rare.

Prickly partnership

Being such solitary creatures, giant pandas do not breed easily. The courtship between a male and female is long and complex. At any point, one of the pandas might do something to frighten the other away.

Pandas breed in spring. A female panda is only able to become pregnant during just one week each year. With such a short time to breed, many giant pandas do not produce young each year.

Once she is pregnant, the female panda looks for a place to give birth. She makes a den in a thicket, in a tree hollow, or in a cave. She lines the den with leaves.

LIFE WITH MOTHER: Males may mate with several females in the breeding season. The females are fertile (produce eggs) only for a short time, and mating often fails to make her pregnant. Panda cubs are born after a five-month gestation. For the first month of their life, they stay in the den with their mother.

Giant panda

MATING SEASON: March–May

GESTATION: 125–150 days

NUMBER OF YOUNG: 1, twins more frequent in captivity

WEIGHT AT BIRTH: 3–3.5 ounces (90–100 g)

EYES OPEN: 7 weeks

FIRST SOLID FOOD: 3 months

SEXUAL MATURITY: 5–7 years

LIFE SPAN: 30 years

Red panda

MATING SEASON: All year

GESTATION: 90–145 days

NUMBER OF YOUNG: 2

WEIGHT AT BIRTH: 4–4.5 ounces (110–130 g)

EYES OPEN: 18 days

FIRST SOLID FOOD: 6 months

SEXUAL MATURITY: 1.5 to 2 years

TOP OF THE WORLD: As it becomes even more independent, the young panda can do everything an adult can, including climbing trees.

OUT AND ABOUT: By six months a panda cub can walk but it also rides on its mother's back.

The life of a giant panda

FENDING FOR ITSELF: At 18 months, the young panda is left by its mother to go off on its own and look after itself.

Only one will do

In the wild, giant pandas generally give birth to a single cub. Twins are more frequent in captivity. The tiny newborn panda is kept safe, tucked under its mother's chin. Panda cubs are born with a long tail, which does not get any longer as the rest of the panda's body grows. An adult's tail is just a furry stump.

By three weeks, the panda cub has grown black-and-white fur. By nine months, the bear has developed the molar teeth needed for eating bamboo.

The cub is still living with its mother during the next breeding season. As the mother prepares to give birth to her next cub, the young panda leaves her side. It can look after itself but will not be able to produce its own young for another four or five years.

CHECK THESE OUT

RELATIVES: • American black bears • Bears, small • **Brown bears** • **Polar bears** • Raccoons
PREDATORS: • Dogs • Leopards

DID YOU KNOW**?**

Tiny offspring

Compared with the size of an adult, giant panda cubs are the smallest of any placental mammal. A male panda might grow to be 285 pounds (130 kg) but it is born weighing just 3 ounces (90 g). Even red panda cubs weigh more than that when they are born.

POLAR BEARS

Polar bears are among the world's largest
meat-eating mammals and are perfectly adapted
to life in the icy Arctic.

Left: *A polar bear stands at the edge of the freezing Arctic waters. Its thick fur coat and layer of fat help protect it from the icy winter temperatures and howling winds. Only the tip of its nose and its footpads are free of fur.*

Polar Hunters

- **COMMON NAME:** Polar bear
- **SCIENTIFIC NAME:** *Ursus maritimus*
- **CLOSELY RELATED SPECIES:** Brown bear, sloth bear, sun bear, American black bear, spectacled bear, and giant panda
- **HABITAT:** Arctic region, including sea ice
- **RANGE:** The Arctic and northern Canada
- **APPEARANCE:** Large bear with creamy-white fur and a dark nose and eyes. The powerful body includes massive shoulders, long limbs, a small head, and long neck. Their huge paws have sharp claws.

P olar bears are huge creatures, competing with the brown bear as the world's largest land carnivore (a group of meat-eating mammals). An adult male polar bear may measure over 8 feet (2.4 m) long and weigh more than 1,540 pounds (700 kg)—as heavy as eight men. The bear's huge paws are the size of dinner plates, measuring 12 inches (30 cm) across, and each one is armed with sharp, curving claws.

Polar bears live in the Arctic. This region, which is within the Arctic Circle at 66.5° north, is mainly an ice-covered ocean, edged by the northernmost parts of North America, Greenland, Scandinavia, and Russia. Polar bears are superbly adapted to life in this harsh habitat—both in and out of water. The coat of thick, creamy-white fur helps keep the bear warm. The long outer hairs are hollow, allowing the sun's rays to reach the skin beneath, which is black. This color absorbs the maximum amount of warmth from the sun.

Strong swimmers

The bear's long snout contains a network of nasal passages, which warm the icy air before it reaches the lungs. Beneath the skin is a thick layer of fatty blubber, which keeps the animal warm when swimming in icy water. Polar bears are equally at home on the sea ice, on land, and in the water. Their scientific name, *Ursus maritimus*, means "sea bear." Features that suit polar bears for swimming

Above: *A polar bear crosses its Arctic habitat, camouflaged and protected by its snowy white coat and a thick, heat-retaining layer of fat.*

RELATIVES

The polar bear is one of eight species of bears in the family Ursidae. Other bears include:

BROWN BEAR (*Ursus arctos*)
Brown bears live in forests and other wild areas across North America, Europe, and Asia. There are several subspecies, including the grizzly bear.

SLOTH BEAR (*Melursus ursinus*)
Sloth bears live in the forests, grasslands, and scrublands of southern Asia, where they eat mainly insects and fruit.

SUN BEAR (*Helarctos malayanus*)
The smallest bear, sun bears live in tropical forests in southeast Asia.

AMERICAN BLACK BEAR (*Ursus americanus*)
Once found throughout North America, black bears now inhabit mainly wilderness areas, mostly in Canada and Alaska.

SPECTACLED BEAR (*Tremarctos ornatus*)
Spectacled bears live on forested slopes of the Andes Mountains in South America. They are named after the markings on their face, which resemble spectacles.

GIANT PANDA (*Ailuropoda melanoleuca*)
Giant pandas feed on bamboo shoots in remote forests in China. These shy animals are now very rare in the wild.

up to 6 miles per hour (10 kph), and can swim nonstop for 100 miles (160 km). Polar bears are often seen far out at sea, beyond sight of land.

Not an average bear

Polar bears are one of eight species of bears now alive on Earth. Bears (family Ursidae) belong to the large group of meat-eating mammals called carnivores, which includes dogs, cats, and stoats. Within this group, bears are most closely related to dogs.

Polar bears have a different diet compared with most bears. While other bears are omnivores, eating both plant and animal foods, polar bears are almost entirely carnivorous (meat eating). They feed mainly on seals, which they catch far out on the ice.

include a small head and a long neck, which produces a sleek, streamlined shape that slips easily through the water. Thick body fat makes the bear naturally buoyant.

Polar bears swim using their front paws, which are partly webbed. Their hind legs either float out behind them as they swim or are held together to

POLAR BEARS ARE OFTEN SEEN FAR OUT AT SEA, BEYOND SIGHT OF LAND.

form a rudder for steering. Polar bears are also expert divers and can remain underwater for up to two minutes. They swim at speeds

Left: *The polar bear and the brown bear share a common ancestor called Ursus etruscus. The polar bear is slightly larger than the brown bear and can swim very strongly in cold waters.*

Below: *The cave bear became extinct at the end of the last ice age, around 10,000 years ago. Just like present-day brown bears, cave bears hibernated during the cold winter months.*

DID YOU KNOW?

Ancestors

Scientists believe that bears and other carnivores are descended from a group of smallish mammals called miacids that lived some 65 million years ago. The first distinctly bearlike carnivores evolved about 25 million years ago, from the same ancestors as dogs. Fossil finds suggest that bears first appeared in Europe about 20 million years ago, and from there spread to other continents, with the exception of Australia and Antarctica.

The earliest known bear, called the dawn bear, was the size of a fox and ate mostly meat. Over millions of years, bears became much larger, and their skulls and teeth became adapted to eating both plant and animal food. Modern bears grew heavier, with shortish limbs and a very short tail. Polar bears are thought to have evolved from brown bears that adapted to living in the Arctic. That adaptation involved switching from an omnivorous diet (including both plant and animal food) to an all-meat diet.

ANATOMY: Polar bear

BROWN BEAR
The brown or grizzly bear has a larger head than the polar bear, with a broad face and large snout.

BLACK BEAR
The American black bear has a narrower head and face than the brown bear, with a shorter, sleeker coat.

Nose
Polar bears have an extremely sharp sense of smell. They are thought to be able to smell a dead seal or whale up to 20 miles (32 km) away.

Neck
The bear's long neck produces a streamlined shape for swimming.

Legs
The polar bear's legs are long and very strong, to support its huge weight. Strong legs allow these bears to cover huge distances as they search for prey.

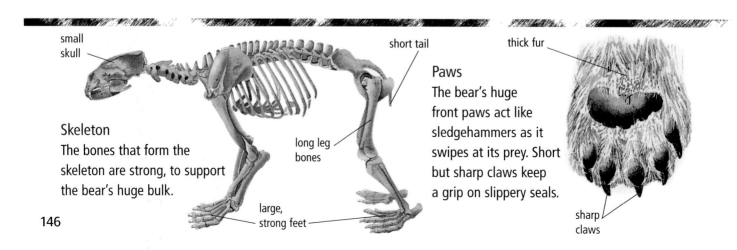

small skull

short tail

thick fur

Skeleton
The bones that form the skeleton are strong, to support the bear's huge bulk.

long leg bones

Paws
The bear's huge front paws act like sledgehammers as it swipes at its prey. Short but sharp claws keep a grip on slippery seals.

large, strong feet

sharp claws

Stomach

Prey is not easy to find in the Arctic. The polar bear has a large stomach that can expand to take in a huge meal that can sustain the bear until it is able to find more food.

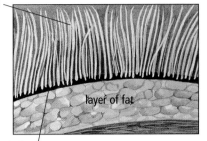

hollow hairs

layer of fat

black skin

Skin and hair

A polar bear's skin is black. The bear looks white because its fur is made of hollow hairs that reflect light from the sun. A thick layer of fat beneath the skin keeps the bear warm.

FACT FILE

The polar bear competes with the brown bear as the world's largest land carnivore. Males grow to 5 feet (1.6 m) high at the shoulder. The smallest bear, the sun bear of southeast Asia (above left), grows to only 2.3 feet (70 cm) tall at the shoulder.

Polar bear

GENUS: *Ursus*
SPECIES: *maritimus*

SIZE

HEAD–BODY LENGTH: Male 6.5–8 feet (2–2.5 m); female 6–6.5 feet (1.8–2 m)
WEIGHT: Male 770–1,540 pounds (350–700 kg); female 330–1,000 pounds (150–450 kg)
WEIGHT AT BIRTH: 1–1.5 pounds (500–700 g)

COLORATION

Varies from pure white in cubs to bluish white, creamy, or yellowish in adults.

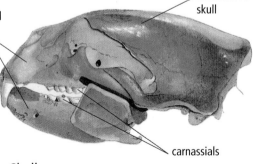

streamlined skull

powerful jaws

carnassials

Teeth

The polar bear's long canine teeth show it to be a true carnivore. Its shearing back teeth, called carnassials, are ideal for the bear's diet of seal meat. These teeth, which slice through flesh, are undeveloped in other bears.

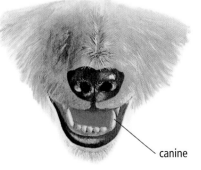

canine

Skull

The skull has a streamlined shape. The polar bear's powerful jaws are used to pull prey from the water. In the case of small whales, this is a huge feat of strength.

A world of ice and snow

Polar bears live throughout the Arctic, but particularly on the pack ice covering the Arctic Ocean. Despite their name, polar bears almost never visit the North Pole itself, since the sea ice is so thick at this most northerly point on Earth that there is very little food there. Beyond the limit of the Arctic Circle, polar bears have been sighted as far south as Iceland, Newfoundland in Canada, and northern Japan.

AMAZING FACTS

• The name "Arctic" comes from the Greek word *arktos* meaning bear—not the polar bear, but the star constellation of the Great Bear (Ursa Major), which shines in the far north.
• When polar bears come out of the water, they shake like dogs to dry their fur.
• Polar bears are so well adapted to the cold that they can easily overheat when running. That is one of the reasons polar bears seldom hunt fast-moving prey.

POLAR BEARS FOLLOW THE PACK ICE AS IT MELTS AND BECOMES SMALLER IN SUMMER.

A changing habitat

The Arctic is a hostile habitat at any time of year but it also sees great seasonal changes. During the brief summer, the sun never sinks below the horizon, so it is light for 24 hours a day. Even at this time, the sun is always low in the sky and so brings little warmth. Average summer temperatures do not rise above 50°F (10°C). During this time, part of the sea ice melts, but ice still covers more than 40 percent of the ocean.

Winter conditions dominate the Arctic for nine months of the year. In midwinter, the sun never rises above the horizon, and it is dark for months on end. Moonlight and the shimmering glow of the aurora borealis (northern lights) provide the only light.

Temperatures may drop as low as –40°F (–40°C), and howling winds increase the chill. In midwinter, ice covers more than 80 percent of the Arctic Ocean. Polar bears in more northerly areas may dig dens in the snow to survive the intense cold.

Following the ice

Polar bears live mostly by hunting seals out on the sea ice. The bears follow the pack ice as it melts and becomes smaller in summer and as it freezes and becomes larger in winter. In southerly parts of the Arctic, bears must move north in summer to stay on the ice or head south to hunt on land.

The pack ice is constantly moving. Pushed by winds and currents, the ice drifts up to 50 miles (80 km) a day in a huge clockwise spiral. To stay in places where there is plenty of food, polar bears have to travel the same distance in the opposite direction. How they find their way in a world where there are no landmarks is a mystery.

Right: *As the ice pack melts in the spring, polar bears have a smaller area in which to hunt.*

Distribution

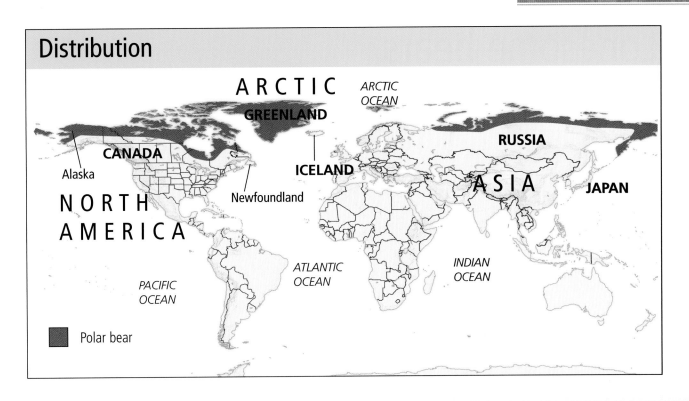

ARCTIC

ARCTIC OCEAN

GREENLAND

RUSSIA

CANADA

ICELAND

ASIA

JAPAN

Alaska

NORTH AMERICA

Newfoundland

ATLANTIC OCEAN

INDIAN OCEAN

PACIFIC OCEAN

Polar bear

Lonesome bears

Polar bears live farther north than any other mammal. People once thought that these bears spent their lives wandering the trackless wastes of the Arctic at random, but radiotracking has shown that their movements follow a more regular pattern.

Home ranges

The total area where an animal roams is called its home range.

In places where the ice is fairly stable, a polar bear's home range is small because it does not have to move far to hunt seals. In areas where the sea ice drifts rapidly or melts in summer, polar bears may have

Top: *This polar bear is following the shifting pack ice as it melts, breaks up, and refreezes.*

Above: *Polar bear cubs closely follow their mother when traveling long distances across the ice and snow.*

to travel hundreds of miles each year as they follow the shifting pack ice. Here, a polar bear's home range may be as large as 100,000 square miles (260,000 sq km).

Scientists are baffled as to how polar bears manage to find their way around such enormous areas. Research suggests that the bears may learn these seasonal movements as cubs, when they follow their mothers for around two and a half years, until they become independent.

Lone rangers

Polar bears mainly live alone, except for females and their cubs. They normally avoid one another unless mating, although they sometimes gather where food is plentiful. Carnivores such as wolves, which spend their lives in a group, have developed complex means of communication, including a wide range of calls, facial expressions, body language, and a system of scent marking. In comparison, polar bears have relatively few calls and facial expressions. Males make a quiet threatening noise which sounds like a cough, called chuffing. Cubs and mothers keep in touch by moaning.

DID YOU KNOW?

Hiding or huddling?

Some Arctic hunters believe that when hunting seals, a polar bear will use its huge paw to hide its black nose to blend in with the snowy landscape. However, there is no direct evidence for this. On the other hand, polar bears have been seen covering their noses with their paws in very cold weather, probably to prevent heat being lost from the nose.

Adjusting to temperatures

Polar bears spend a great deal of their time asleep, which helps conserve energy. They sometimes sleep using blocks of ice as pillows or in a daybed, made by scooping out snow.

Resting bears adopt different positions to keep warm in very cold weather or to cool off during the "heat" of the Arctic summer. On warm days, they sprawl or lie on their backs with their paws in the air. In cold weather, they curl up. Unlike bears living in warmer regions farther south, polar bears do not hibernate in winter, although females hole up in dens with their cubs.

Below: *This pregnant female polar bear has dug out a den in a snowdrift behind a bank of earth. Protected from the cold and bitter wind outside, she will give birth to her cubs here.*

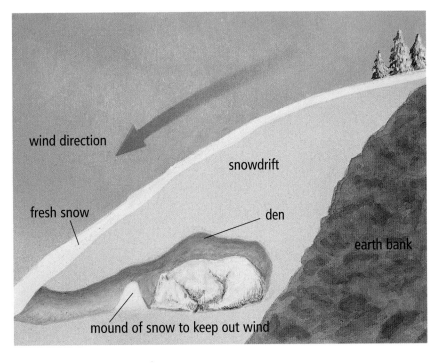

wind direction

snowdrift

fresh snow

den

earth bank

mound of snow to keep out wind

Skillful hunters

Polar bears are the most carnivorous of all bears. Their favorite prey by far are ringed seals, but polar bears also hunt harp seals and hooded seals, particularly the pups.

Left: *This resourceful polar bear shows remarkable patience as it lies in wait by a seal's breathing hole. The bear lies on its stomach on the ice, inching closer and closer to the hole as quietly as possible, until it is in prime position to pounce. This technique is called still-hunting.*

Lurking

Polar bears are versatile hunters that use different techniques to catch their prey. One of their favorite methods is called still-hunting. The bear lies by a hole in the sea ice, which seals use to breathe, and waits patiently until a seal surfaces. Then the polar bear lunges forward, biting its prey and throwing it out onto the ice. It kills the seal by biting its head and neck or with a swipe of its huge paws.

Den raiding

In spring, polar bears hunt seal pups in their dens in the ice. A keen sense of smell allows the bear to detect a seal pup up to 0.6 mile (1 km) away. On reaching the den, the polar bear rears up on its pwerful hind legs and crashes down with all its weight to break through the ice roof of the den.

Above and right: *A polar bear sniffs the air to locate prey (**1**). Rising up on its hind legs, the polar bear lifts its powerful forepaws high in the air, ready to pounce (**2**). Dropping all of its weight through the thick ice roof, the bear gets its meal (**3**).*

Left: *A polar bear spots a stranded beluga whale. With one leap, the bear rushes toward its victim, slashing it with sharp claws and dragging it onto the ice before eating it.*

Stalking

In summer, when adult seals bask on the ice, polar bears approach them by stalking. The bear creeps slowly forward, sometimes in a crouched position, until it is about 75 feet (22 m) away, and then makes a sudden charge.

Other food items

As well as seals, polar bears also hunt marine mammals as large as beluga whales. In summer, when the ice melts in southerly regions, polar bears hunt voles and lemmings on the tundra (treeless plains).

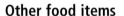

They may raid colonies of nesting birds to seize females and their eggs. Polar bears have been known to tackle prey as large as musk oxen. They also eat carrion (dead animals).

In summer, polar bears eat grass, berries, and seaweed.

PREY

Seals make up over 90 percent of the diet of most polar bears, but the bears also hunt other prey, including:

RINGED SEAL (*Pusa hispida*)
This seal is the most abundant marine mammal in the Arctic.

HOODED SEAL (*Cystophora cristata*)
In spring, polar bears hunt hooded seal and harp seal pups in their lairs.

BELUGA (*Delphinapterus leucas*)
Polar bears kill small whales called belugas when the whales get trapped at breathing holes in winter or stranded in rivers in summer.

EIDER DUCK (*Somateria mollissima*)
Polar bears attack waterfowl on their nests or swim beneath ducks and pull them under.

LEMMING (subfamily Arvicolinae)
In summer, small rodents such as lemmings and voles fall prey to polar bears.

Fierce competition

Polar bears are slow breeders. Females give birth only once every three years, producing between 4 and 10 cubs in their lifetimes. During the breeding season, competition over females is fierce. If two or more males come across a female, a violent fight breaks out. The winner stays with the female for a week or more and mates with her several times.

Breeding and birth

Polar bears mate in late April and May, but the fertilized egg does not begin to grow until October. By this time, the pregnant female has moved north to the denning area where she will give birth to her cubs. She digs a den in a snowdrift toward the end of October and gives birth in late December or early January. Seventy-five percent of females give birth to twins, with a single cub or triplets being rarer.

The life of a polar bear

RIDING HIGH: When traveling across deep snow or crossing a bay, the cub often climbs onto its mother's back and clings on tightly with its sharp claws.

Polar bear

MATING SEASON: Late April to May

GESTATION: 195–265 days

NUMBER OF YOUNG: 1–3, normally twins

WEIGHT AT BIRTH: 1–1.5 pounds (500–700 g)

EYES OPEN: By 1 month old

LEAVE DEN: Around 3 months

FIRST SOLID FOOD: 5 months

INDEPENDENCE: By 2 years

SEXUAL MATURITY: 4–5 years

LIFE SPAN: 18–30 years in the wild, up to 41 years in captivity

Tiny, helpless cubs

Newborn polar bear cubs are tiny compared with the huge bulk of their mother. They are blind, deaf, and covered with thin white fur. The female keeps the cubs warm with her body and suckles them on her milk, which is the richest of any land mammal. Nourished by this high-fat food, the offspring grow quickly. At one month old, they can see and hear. At two months, they begin to explore inside the den.

Growing up

Between March and April, the female comes out of the den with her cubs. The offspring are naturally curious. They play in the snow, chase around in circles, and slide down slopes. By now, the female is very hungry because she has not eaten for many months. She leads her cubs down to the frozen sea, where there are plenty of seals. When they reach the sea, the cubs learn by watching their mother hunt and copying her actions. At two years old, the cubs are able to hunt.

They stay with their mother until she lets them leave or until they are frightened away by a male who wants to mate with her. Polar bears normally live to about 18 years but have been known to survive for 32 years in the wild and to 41 years in captivity.

RICH DIET: The mother suckles the tiny cubs regularly inside the den. Her rich milk helps them grow quickly.

SPRING BREAK: In spring, the mother breaks out of the den and the three-month-old cubs start to explore their surroundings.

CLOSE FAMILY: The cubs stay close to their mother for the first few months and continue to suckle until the age of two.

Skating on thin ice

In the past, hunting was the main threat to polar bears. Now new dangers have appeared that threaten the Arctic generally: pollution and global warming.

Arctic groups of people, such as the Inuit, traditionally hunted polar bears for meat and because the bears competed for the main food of local people—seals. The Inuit hunted the bears using teams of dogs, which distracted the bear while the hunters launched their spears. For centuries, hunting with spears posed no real threat to the survival of polar bears as a species, but from the sixteenth century, southerners arrived with rifles. Larger numbers of polar bears were then killed.

Trophy hunters

In the centuries that followed, explorers and trappers killed increasing numbers of bears for meat and, later, for trophies. In the twentieth century, trophy-hunters used airplanes and snowmobiles to track the bears. However, public opinion turned against hunting and, in 1973, a general ban on polar bear hunting was agreed by Arctic nations. The only exceptions are the hunting of a few bears each year by native hunters, for scientific research, and in self-defence.

Environmental dangers

Hunting is no longer a threat to polar bears, but new problems have surfaced. Pollution and loss of habitat both threaten the Arctic wilderness. Pollution comes from mining, particularly of oil in Alaska and Siberia, and also

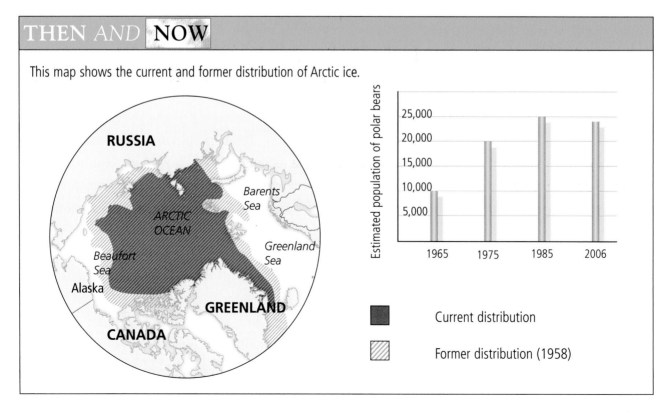

THEN *AND* NOW

This map shows the current and former distribution of Arctic ice.

RUSSIA

Barents
Sea

ARCTIC
OCEAN

Beaufort
Sea

Greenland
Sea

Alaska

GREENLAND

CANADA

Estimated population of polar bears

25,000
20,000
15,000
10,000
5,000

1965   1975   1985   2006

Current distribution

Former distribution (1958)

from chemicals such as pesticides, used in farming, which end up in the ocean. Here, the poisons are absorbed by plankton (floating microorganisms) and pass up the food chain to fish, seals, and—finally—polar bears.

Global warming is a serious threat to the Arctic and its wildlife. Increased levels of greenhouse gases such as carbon dioxide in Earth's atmosphere are causing more of the sun's heat to be trapped near the planet. Polar habitats are being more affected by this warming than other areas.

The ice of the Arctic Ocean is now 40 percent thinner than it was 40 years ago and covers 5 percent less of the ocean.

Above: *A polar bear guards its kill on an ice floe. Global warming is causing the ice to melt more quickly, which makes it difficult for polar bears to hunt.*

The melting ice makes it more difficult for polar bears to hunt, and as warming continues, their habitat is shrinking. The ice is melting three weeks earlier each spring, which means three weeks less feeding time for polar bears every year.

In the twentieth century, national parks and preserves, such as the Arctic National Wildlife Refuge (ANWR), were set up in Alaska and Canada to protect Arctic habitats. However, some of these untouched areas are threatened by new mining plans.

At risk

The International Union for the Conservation of Nature (IUCN) defines the threat to polar bears as follows:

POLAR BEAR	*Lower risk*

However, polar bears may move into a category of higher risk if present trends continue. Pollution, global warming, and new mining plans all pose significant threats to the whole Arctic habitat, and thus to the future of polar bears.

CHECK THESE OUT
RELATIVES: • American brown bears • **Brown bears** • **Pandas** • Small bears PREY: • **Seals, true** • Right whales • Voles and lemmings

SEALS, TRUE

Graceful and streamlined, true seals are agile and fast swimmers, capable of diving to depths of hundreds of feet and staying underwater for up to an hour. They live mainly in the polar, subpolar, and temperate seas, preying on fish, squid, octopuses, shellfish, and in the case of leopard seals, on penguins and other seals.

Right: *A gray seal has hauled itself onto an ice floe after diving for squid, crabs, and fish, such as cod, flatfish, herring, and mackerel. Its thick layer of blubber protects it from the freezing temperatures.*

Below: *Resting on a beach, this bull elephant seal is surrounded by his harem of females and their pups.*

Swimmers with Stamina

In 1494, two years after crossing the Atlantic Ocean from Europe, Italian navigator and explorer Christopher Columbus (1451–1506) and his expedition were exploring the Caribbean islands. He ordered his crew to slaughter eight "sea wolves" for their supper. In doing so, he was correct in identifying Caribbean monk seals both as mammals and as carnivores. Carnivores belong to the order of mammals called Carnivora, which includes wolves.

Most seal experts believe that seals evolved from carnivore ancestors within the last 20 to 30 million years.

There are three groups of seals: eared seals, true seals, and the walrus. Seals once were classified in a suborder of mammals called Pinnipedia, meaning "wing-footed." This name refers to their wing-shaped forelimbs, which are paddles called flippers. Seals and their relatives are therefore called pinnipeds but are now grouped under the order Carnivora.

True (or earless) seals are called "true" because they were the first seals to be described by scientists. They are also called "earless" because they do not have visible external ears. Their internal ears are, however, fully

RELATIVES

True seals include harbor, or common, seals, elephant seals, hooded seals, and monk seals. They are related to the walrus and to the 16 species of eared seals.

WALRUS (*Odobenus rosmarus*)
Living mainly in the coastal waters of the Arctic Ocean and adjoining seas, male walruses are enormous: up to 11.5 feet (3.5 m) long and 3,750 pounds (1,700 kg) in weight. The long tusks are a well-known feature of the adult animal.

NORTHERN FUR SEAL (*Callorhinus ursinus*)
These eared seals live in the north Pacific Ocean, mainly in the coastal waters, on offshore rocks, islands, and beaches. They feed on fish, krill, lobsters, and occasionally penguins. Fur seal pups are sometimes eaten by sea lions.

CALIFORNIA SEA LION (*Zalophus californianus*)
These animals live on the Pacific coast and in the Gulf of California, from Canada to Baja California. The males are usually dark chestnut brown, around 8 feet (2.4 m) long, and weigh up to 600 pounds (275 kg). The females are tan colored and around one-third the size of the male.

functional. They can hear well both above and below the water.

The 18 living species of true seals belong to the family Phocidae. A 19th species, the Caribbean monk seal, the type that Columbus described as a "sea wolf," probably no longer exists. After centuries of hunting, the last specimens were seen in the 1950s.

Fossil evidence reveals that true seals originated in the northeast of the Atlantic Ocean some 25 million years ago. From there, ancestors spread north and south, encircling the globe from pole to pole. They live mainly in colder waters that have a good food supply.

Belonging to the family Otariidae are 16 species of eared seals, such as sea lions and fur seals. Unlike true seals,

Above: *The harbor seal, or common seal, is one of several species of white-coated seals. It is extremely widespread, from the Baltic Sea and across the Atlantic and Pacific oceans as far south as southern Japan.*

Right: *It is obvious why the hooded seal is so named; it has a nose hood, or pouch, that it can inflate, possibly to attract a partner or scare off a rival.*

DID YOU KNOW?

Little and large

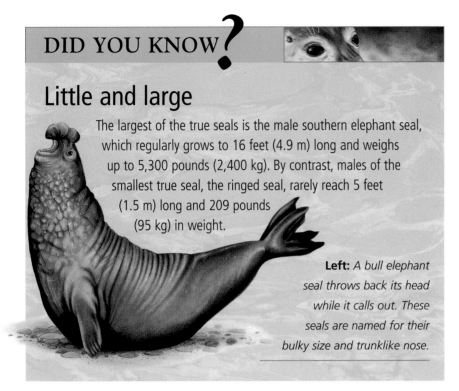

The largest of the true seals is the male southern elephant seal, which regularly grows to 16 feet (4.9 m) long and weighs up to 5,300 pounds (2,400 kg). By contrast, males of the smallest true seal, the ringed seal, rarely reach 5 feet (1.5 m) long and 209 pounds (95 kg) in weight.

Left: *A bull elephant seal throws back its head while it calls out. These seals are named for their bulky size and trunklike nose.*

eared seals have visible ears. They differ from true seals in a number of other ways, including how they move around in water and on land.

The third family of seals, Odobenidae, has only one species, the walrus. The walrus has some similarities to true seals and other resemblances to eared seals.

Eared seals are built for speed and maneuverability in the water. They move themselves along with fore flippers, using a rowing action. Their chests are broad and their fore flippers strong. On land they can move around quite well. By rotating their hind flippers forward and using their fore flippers as props, they can walk, although somewhat awkwardly.

Flipper power

True seals, on the other hand, are streamlined almost to perfection. They are built for efficiency and endurance in the water. True seals can dive deeper and for longer periods than eared seals. A true seal's fore flippers are small and it usually tucks them away when swimming. It drives itself forward with hind flippers, first extending one hind flipper and drawing it back in and then extending the other. At the same time, the seal moves the rear half of its body from side to side. The overall effect is like that of a fish, with its tail moving from side to side, and it is very nearly as effective.

On land, however, true seals are much clumsier than eared seals. Their fore flippers are too small to act as effective props and they cannot swing their hind flippers forward, as eared seals do. Instead of walking, they hump themselves along on their bellies. Some biologists describe this action as galumphing, taken from Lewis Carroll's word for clumsy movement in the nonsense poem *Jabberwocky*.

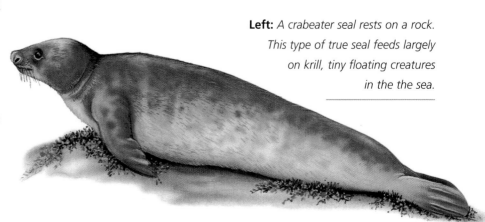

Left: *A crabeater seal rests on a rock. This type of true seal feeds largely on krill, tiny floating creatures in the the sea.*

ANATOMY: Harbor seal

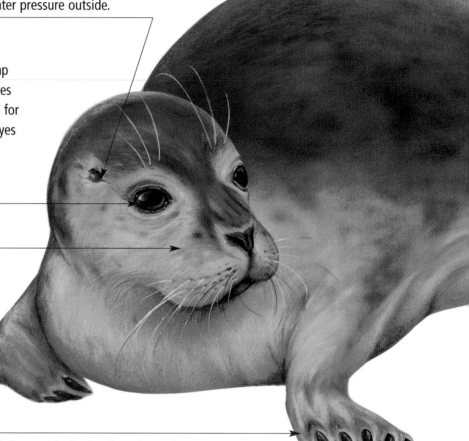

Ears
The ears have no external flaps. Nevertheless, the ears are highly sensitive to sounds underwater. To prevent the eardrum from becoming damaged when diving, chambers in the ear inflate with blood. This balances the air pressure inside with the increase in water pressure outside.

Eyes
The large eyes face forward. The overlap in the field of view of the two eyes gives the seal good three-dimensional vision for judging distances when hunting. The eyes see well underwater, even in dim light, but focus much less well when the seal is looking through air.

Muzzle
The muzzle has long, sensitive whiskers that help detect prey in murky water. The whiskers are sensitive to touch and to pressure waves produced by objects moving close to the muzzle, including fish.

Fore flippers
The short, clawed fore flippers are held close to the body when the seal is swimming fast. At slow speeds they help steer the seal. Claws enable some species, including the harbor seal, to hold large prey while tearing off large chunks with their teeth, like an otter does.

Body
The sleek, streamlined body has a thin covering of hairs, but most of the insulation against heat loss comes from the thick layer of blubber beneath the skin.

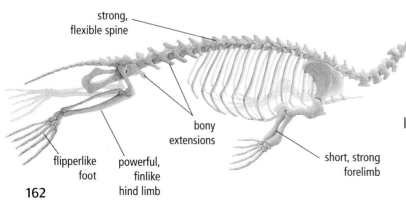

strong,
flexible spine

flipperlike
foot

powerful,
finlike
hind limb

bony
extensions

short, strong
forelimb

Skeleton
The backbone, made up of bony units called vertebrae, is extremely flexible. That allows the seal to move its body from side to side while swimming. The lower back (lumbar) vertebrae are strong and have bony extensions above and to the sides, to which powerful muscles for swimming are attached.

Hind flippers

Like all true seals of the northern subfamily, the harbor seal has large claws on its hind flippers, although they have little function because the hind flippers are used mostly for swimming. On southern true seals, such as the elephant seal, the claws are hardly present at all, and the toes are strongly webbed. This webbing makes the hind flippers much better at pushing the animal through the water.

reduced claws, more webbing between toes

ELEPHANT SEAL

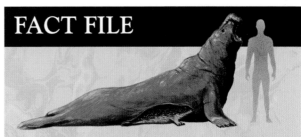
claws on hind flipper

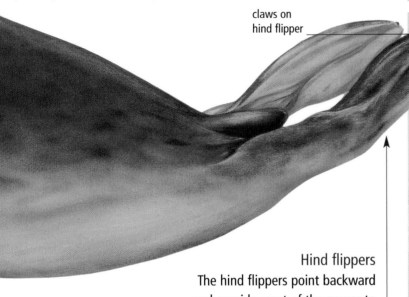

Hind flippers

The hind flippers point backward and provide most of the power to propel the seal through the water. The seal skulls with them, first on one side and then the other.

ELEPHANT SEAL

LEOPARD SEAL

HARBOR SEAL

Harbor seal

GENUS: *Phoca*
SPECIES: *vitulina*

SIZE

HEAD–BODY LENGTH: Male up to 75 inches (190 cm); female up to 67 inches (170 cm)
WEIGHT: Male up to 370 pounds (170 kg); female up to 290 pounds (130 kg)

COLORATION

Adult ranges from light tan or silver to dark gray, with dense mottling of darker spots or rings; pups have a pale fur that is shed before birth and replaced by fur similar to that of the adult.

Head shapes

The rounded, doglike head and large eyes of the harbor seal (left) are typical true seal features. The leopard seal (center) has exceptionally strong jaws for handling penguins and small seals as prey. The enlarged muzzle of the male elephant seal (far left) makes its roars much louder.

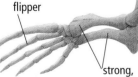

flipper

shoulder blade

strong, sturdy bones

Forelimb

The seal's forelimb is short with strong sturdy bones.

Skull and lower jaw

The daggerlike incisor teeth at the front of the jaw are used for stabbing and grasping prey. The cheek teeth have less of a slicing action than those of land-living carnivores. Seals eat their prey whole or in large chunks.

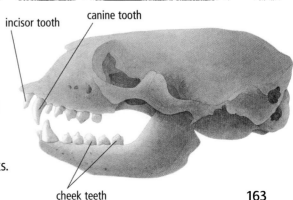

incisor tooth

canine tooth

cheek teeth

Oceans to ice

Like eared seals and the walrus, all true seals get their food from the oceans but they must come to land—or at least floating ice—to mate, give birth, and, in many cases, to suckle their offspring.

True seals live across the world, from balmy seas to freezing waters. Monk seals favor mild, temperate waters, but most true-seal species live in cooler waters.

> **ALL TRUE SEALS GET THEIR FOOD FROM THE OCEANS BUT THEY MUST COME TO LAND TO MATE, GIVE BIRTH, AND TO SUCKLE THEIR OFFSPRING.**

The largest gatherings of true seals occur in polar or subpolar waters. Here, the waters in summer are rich in fish and shrimplike animals called krill, which are the favored foods of most true seals.

In Antarctica and on subantarctic islands there are no land predators to attack seal pups on beaches. However, when pups enter the water they may be at the mercy of killer

Below: *A harbor seal and her pup rest on some floating ice. Although there is a strong bond between mother and pup, harbor seals generally avoid close contact with other seals.*

Distribution

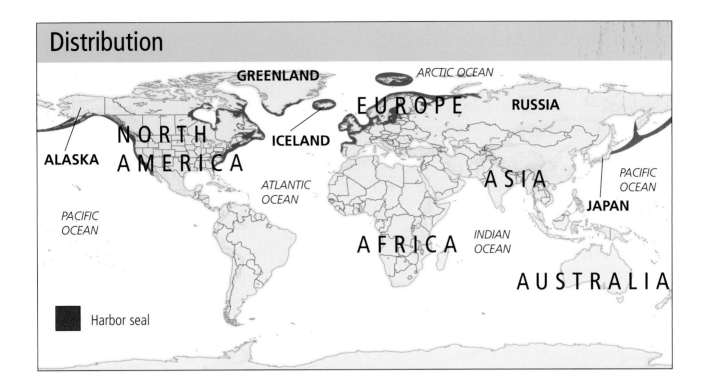

GREENLAND

ARCTIC OCEAN

EUROPE

RUSSIA

NORTH
AMERICA

ICELAND

ALASKA

ATLANTIC
OCEAN

ASIA

PACIFIC
OCEAN

JAPAN

PACIFIC
OCEAN

AFRICA

INDIAN
OCEAN

AUSTRALIA

Harbor seal

whales and leopard seals. Killer whales have been known to knock seals off ice floes and into the water, where they are snatched by other whales in the group.

In the Arctic, predators such as polar bears and arctic foxes can make their way from the land onto pack ice. Polar bears and humans wait at breathing holes in the ice to pounce on seals when they rise to breathe. Seals make breathing holes by cutting through the ice with their teeth.

Bears and foxes can sniff out a seal pup in its den in the ice. Nevertheless, floating ice can be a relatively safe haven for seals. As global warming takes place, loss of sea ice could make life much more difficult for the populations of Arctic seals.

Blubber layer

All true seals have a thick layer of blubber for heat insulation. It keeps the body warmth in and the penetrating chill of icy waters out. Even warm-water seals have thick blubber. Part of the reason is that at depths below the top 330 to 660 feet (100–200 m), ocean water is cold, whether in tropical or polar seas. Thus the surrounding water temperature beyond this depth is likely to be less than 50°F (10°C) and much cooler than the warm body temperature of a seal, which is at least 95°F (35°C).

AMAZING FACTS

• The crabeater seal of Antarctic waters is the most abundant of all seals. It numbers more than 10 million.

• The crabeater's cheek teeth work like sieves, filtering small animal plankton, such as krill, out of the water it gulps.

• The numbers of crabeater seals has dramatically increased since the mid-twentieth century because of the decline of baleen whale populations caused by whaling. Baleen whales compete with crabeater seals for krill. With fewer whales around, there is more food for the seals.

Keeping to the seas

Right: *These bull elephant seals are fighting to secure a territory on the beach. They are enormously powerful and use brute strength to establish their dominance. The winner not only gains the territory but also gets the right to mate with all the females on the beach. Therefore, there is a great deal at stake for these males.*

Although true seals come ashore or gather on pack ice to breed or molt, most spend more than three-quarters of their lives at sea. When they do come ashore, their movements are awkward and they are vulnerable to attacks from land predators. Therefore they keep their time out of the water to a minimum. To achieve this, mothers give birth and suckle their offspring as quickly as possible.

The hooded seal and harbor seal have taken this behavior to extremes. The hooded seal mother of North Atlantic waters suckles her pup on incredibly fat- and protein-rich milk for only three to five days before leaving it to develop further on its own. A harbor seal mother usually gives birth

DID YOU KNOW?

Controlling blood to the skin

True seals and walruses can control the blood flow to the skin. When diving in cold water, they contract blood vessels near the skin's surface, so reducing heat loss through the skin. On land, they expand these blood vessels to pick up heat from the sun's rays or to cool off if they get too hot while on land to breed and feed their offspring.

into its watery surroundings. To molt, the seal comes ashore or clambers onto ice, where less heat is lost to the air. Polar species time their molting so that it happens in summer, when the seals can bask in 24-hour sunshine.

In places where seals are forced to molt in chilly air, as happens with some elephant seal populations, the animals pack together tightly to gain heat from each other and keep out the bitter cold.

to her pup on the strandline of a beach at low tide. When the tide rises a few hours later, she escorts her pup into the water and suckles it there.

Molting ashore

True seals also come ashore to molt. Each year a seal sheds and renews its coat of hair. This process of molting and regrowth requires blood to be diverted to the skin. Were this to happen in water, the seal would lose far too much heat

DID YOU KNOW?

Designed for diving

Seals have a variety of features that enable them to dive deep and stay underwater for long periods. The Weddell seal sets the record, with scientists monitoring one individual diving to more than 1,600 feet (500 m) for over an hour.

Just before a deep dive, a seal takes in a large lungful of air, which charges its blood with oxygen. It then breathes out just as it dives, so reducing its buoyancy and expelling waste carbon dioxide. In its bloodstream and muscles are rich chemical stores of trapped oxygen, which the seal gradually uses up during a dive.

When diving deep, the seal's heart rate slows to only four or five beats a minute. The seal greatly reduces blood flow to all but the most essential organs, such as the brain and heart. In this way it keeps oxygen consumption to a minimum. On surfacing, the seal's heart rate and breathing rate rise above normal as it recharges its oxygen supplies in preparation for the next dive.

Different seals, assorted prey

Most true seals feed on small fish and animal plankton, such as krill, which they grab and swallow whole or in large chunks. Seal species in the Antarctic Ocean illustrate the wide range of feeding techniques used by true seals.

Weddell seals of the Antarctic Ocean are superb deep-divers and hunt beneath the sheets of sea ice that grow out from the Antarctic continent. A Weddell seal uses its teeth to carve out a breathing hole in the ice and returns to this hole at the end of each dive. It usually dives for 8 to 15 minutes at a time and then returns to breathe air for 2 to 4 minutes before diving again. A fast swimmer, it can catch even agile fish, such as Antarctic cod. It has good eyesight in dim light and senses vibrations in the water with its whiskers.

Above: A leopard seal chases after newly weaned crabeater seal pups. These young seals are extremely vulnerable to attack because they are inexperienced and clumsy in the water.

The Ross seal also hunts under sheet ice. Its prey are squid and the seal has large eyes to find them. In dim light, it is helped by bioluminescence —self-generated light produced by some squid.

The crabeater seal is unusual in having teeth with very long cusps (projections). When the teeth in the two jaws are brought together, the cusps form a meshwork that works like a net. The seal gulps in a mouthful of water, straining it out through its teeth, and traps animal plankton on them.

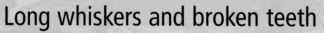

DID YOU KNOW?

Long whiskers and broken teeth

The bearded seal of the Arctic gets its name from its long whiskers. These touch-sensitive hairs help the seal find fish, shrimp, crabs, and clams on the sea bottom in dim light. Most elderly bearded seals have worn and broken teeth after years spent biting through the hard shells of prey.

Below: *This leopard seal is preying on penguins. Leopard seals usually surprise their victims by hiding under the edges of the ice and between floes.*

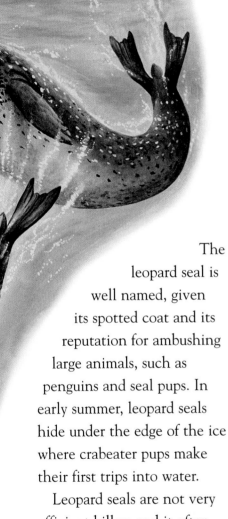

PREY

Although most true seals feed on small fish and animal plankton, leopard seals also eat penguins and seal pups.

CRABEATER SEAL (*Lobodon carcinophagus*)
When they first enter the water, crabeater seal pups are particularly vulnerable to leopard seals.

PENGUIN (family Spheniscidae)
By hiding under an ice floe, a leopard seal can surprise penguins as they swim by. These birds provide an excellent source of protein for the seals.

COD (family Gadidae)
Cod are large fish that live throughout the Atlantic and Antarctic oceans.

PREDATORS

True seals are expert predators but they often fall prey to some of the ocean's largest hunters.

KILLER WHALE (*Orcinus orca*)
A large male killer whale can eat up to 220 pounds (100 kg) of food a day, the equivalent of four seal pups or 400 herring.

POLAR BEAR (*Ursus maritimus*)
A polar bear can sniff out a seal pup even beneath thick ice in its birth lair. The bear is heavy enough and strong enough to crash through the ice to reach the helpless pup within. Polar bears also lie in wait by the breathing holes made by seals. As soon as the seal surfaces, the polar bear pounces.

The leopard seal is well named, given its spotted coat and its reputation for ambushing large animals, such as penguins and seal pups. In early summer, leopard seals hide under the edge of the ice where crabeater pups make their first trips into water.

Leopard seals are not very efficient killers and it often takes several bites and much thrashing in the water to slay the victim.

By specializing in eating different types of food, the true seals of the Antarctic Ocean exist alongside one another without taking each other's food supplies.

Below: *Crabeater seals feed on krill from the sea using their sievelike teeth. The heavily cusped teeth mesh together to strain out the tiny creatures from the water.*

Defending the beaches

As eared seals do, the adult males of true seals establish territories in which they seek to mate with all the resident females. However, in true seals these territories may be in the water rather than on beaches. Adult male Weddell seals, for example, claim as their territory the water beneath several breathing holes in the ice. Any male or female that swims into this territory is waylaid. If male, the intruder is seen off. If female, she is courted to stay and mate.

Beach territories

Among true seals, adult male gray seals and northern elephant seals establish territories on beaches.

During the breeding season, a male gray seal landing on a beach that is occupied by females immediately seeks to establish and defend a territory, warning off other male gray seals that try to intrude.

Inflated threats

Adult male northern elephant seals take the establishment and defense of a territory to extremes. Male elephant seals are extremely bulky, weighing about three times as much as adult females. Males have long canine teeth,

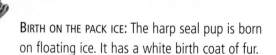

BIRTH ON THE PACK ICE: The harp seal pup is born on floating ice. It has a white birth coat of fur.

The life of a harp seal

JOSTLING FOR POSITION: Nearly a year after mating, the female has to bully her way to find a place on the pack ice where she can give birth to her next pup.

like miniature tusks, which they use for fighting. The neck and chest are covered with tough wrinkled skin. A short, trunklike structure on the snout can be inflated; it looks intimidating and magnifies the sound of the seal's snorts and roars. Males charge each other and throw the upper body on the other, seeking to use brute force to make the rival back down.

The male hooded seal can close his nostrils and force air into a nose cavity, making it swell like a black balloon to attract a female. Alternatively, he can close one nostril, and force air into the other, inflating a membrane that looks like a glossy red balloon, which acts as a threat display to other males.

> ## Harp seal
> **GESTATION:** 50 weeks
> **LENGTH AT BIRTH:** Around 33 inches (85 cm)
> **WEIGHT AT BIRTH:** 24–26 pounds (11–12 kg)
> **WEANING PERIOD:** 10–12 days
> **WEIGHT AT WEANING:** 70–73 pounds (32–33 kg)
> **FIRST SWIM:** 26 days
> **SEXUAL MATURITY:** 5–6 years
> **LIFE SPAN:** 30 years or more

Female fat reserves

The way that true seals suckle and rear their offspring is very different to that of eared seals. Female true seals do all or most of their feeding before they get to the breeding grounds. They build up enormous fat reserves, and each mother gives her newborn calf extremely thick, fat-rich milk. On average, the females of most species of true seals aim to spend three weeks on the breeding beaches. In that time a mother gives birth, suckles her pup to the point where it is weaned, and mates again. Northern elephant seal mothers suckle their young for about 28 days before they leave them to fend for themselves. In hooded seals of the North Atlantic, the suckling period is only three to five days, a record among mammals. Once mothers have left their offspring, the pups stay on the breeding beaches or ice floes until they are developed enough to swim and then hunt for themselves. Until this point, they have to rely on the stored nourishment from the milk they drank from their mother days or weeks previously.

WEANING: The pup is suckled for only 10 to 14 days, at which point the mother leaves.

MOLTING: The pup's pale coat is shed before it takes its first swim.

Blood on the ice

People have hunted true seals for thousands of years, but only in the last few centuries has this hunting changed from small-scale for a family's or community's needs to large-scale hunting for profit. Adult true seals may not have the thick, luxuriant fur of some eared seals but the pups of some northern species do have rich fur. In addition, adult seal skin is a sound weatherproof covering used to make clothes. Almost all parts of the seal can be used, whether it is the meat for food, fat for candles, or sinews for thread.

The harp seal of the North Atlantic Ocean was the first true seal to be exploited for money. Beginning with Basque whalers taking seals off the coasts of Newfoundland in the sixteenth century, commercial seal hunting increased until the mid-nineteenth century, when tens of thousands of seals were taken in the North Atlantic each year.

By the mid-twentieth century, hundreds of thousands of harp seals were killed annually. Seal experts estimate that 50 million harp seals were taken by hunters during the nineteenth and twentieth centuries. It is surprising that harp seal populations have survived as well as they have. Other species of true seals have not done so well.

Competition for fish

Apart from their value as a source of meat, oil, and fur, seals are commonly seen by fishers as competitors for their fish catch. Until recently, fishers in many parts of the world routinely killed any seals they encountered at sea.

Hunting and persecution by fishers has driven at least one species of true seal—the Caribbean monk seal—to extinction. Two species of monk seals—the Mediterranean and the Hawaiian species—remain highly endangered. They have a strong chance of becoming extinct within decades.

Pollution

Seals also have other challenges to deal with. Pollution is taking its toll on seals in some coastal waters. Poisonous heavy metals, such as lead and mercury, pesticides (chemicals used to

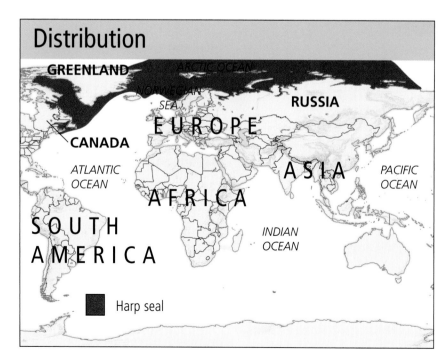

Distribution

GREENLAND
ARCTIC OCEAN
NORWEGIAN SEA
RUSSIA
EUROPE
CANADA
ATLANTIC OCEAN
ASIA
PACIFIC OCEAN
AFRICA
SOUTH AMERICA
INDIAN OCEAN

Harp seal

kill insects), and other toxic substances get washed into the sea. There, they accumulate in fish and other animals, and are passed on to seals when they eat contaminated prey. Deaths of ringed and gray seals in the Baltic Sea and of harbor seals in the North Sea have been linked to pollutants.

Through overfishing, fishers are removing the food that seals might eat. In parts of the North Atlantic Ocean, seals have left their old hunting grounds because fishers have taken so many fish. Far from seals depriving the fishers of catch, the reverse applies.

Mediterranean problems

The Mediterranean monk seal is the world's most endangered seal. The population of 400 to 500 animals is thinly scattered across the Mediterranean region, from northwestern

At risk

This chart shows how the International Union for the Conservation of Nature (IUCN) classifies true seals:

MEDITERRANEAN MONK SEAL	*Critically endangered*
HAWAIIAN MONK SEAL	*Endangered*
CARIBBEAN MONK SEAL	*Extinct*
CASPIAN SEAL	*Vulnerable*
HOODED SEAL, BEARDED SEAL, GRAY SEAL, RIBBON SEAL, LEOPARD SEAL, WEDDELL SEAL, CRABEATER SEAL, NORTHERN ELEPHANT SEAL, SOUTHERN ELEPHANT SEAL, ROSS SEAL, BAIKAL SEAL, HARP SEAL, SPOTTED SEAL, RINGED SEAL, AND HARBOR SEAL	*Least concern*

Critically endangered means that this species faces an extremely high risk of extinction in the wild. *Endangered* means that this species faces a very high risk of extinction in the wild. *Vulnerable* means that the species faces a high risk of extinction in the wild in the future if nothing is done. *Extinct* means that there is no doubt that the last individual has died. *Least concern* means that the species does not qualify for any other category.

Below: *A harp seal pup is camouflaged against the ice. Although harp seals have been hunted extensively over the last few hundred years, these true seals are not under threat.*

Africa to Croatia and Turkey, with many gaps in between. Hunted for thousands of years, this seal is still seen by some fishers as an unwelcome competitor for fish, which have been decimated by decades of overfishing. Some fishers illegally shoot these protected seals. They are also threatened by water pollution and by becoming entangled in nets set for fish. The outlook for these rare seals remains bleak.

CHECK THESE OUT
RELATIVES: • Seals, eared
PREDATORS: • **Killer whales** • **Polar bears**

TIGERS

Tigers are the largest cats alive. They live in the grasslands, swamps, and forests of Asia, where they are silent but deadly killers. The tigers' most familiar features, their orange, white, and black striped coats, provide excellent camouflage among the tall grass and undergrowth.

Left: *A tiger is a large, powerfully built cat. Tigers usually prey on animals much larger than themselves, such as deer and cattle. Tigers have relatively short but very muscular forelimbs and large paws with long, sharp claws to grab their prey and hang on.*

Right: *The markings on the face of a tiger are as unique as a person's fingerprints.*

Below: *This tiger is a white tiger, a mutant form of the orange Bengal tiger or a mixture of Bengal and Amur tigers. White tigers usually have a pink nose, white to cream fur, and black, gray, or chocolate-colored stripes. These tigers are born when close relatives interbreed, such as a mother and a son or a sister and a brother.*

- **COMMON NAME:** Tiger
- **SCIENTIFIC NAME:** *Panthera tigris*
- **SUBSPECIES:** Six subspecies are recognized, although some may simply be the result of environmental or geographic variations: Bengal tiger (*Panthera tigris tigris*), South China tiger (*P. t. amoyensis*), Indo-Chinese tiger (*P. t. corbetti*), Sumatran tiger (*P. t. sumatrae*), Amur tiger (*P. t. altaica*), and Malayan tiger (*P. t. jacksonii*)
- **HABITAT:** Grasslands, swamps, and forests
- **RANGE:** From eastern Russia through parts of China, India, and southeast Asia
- **APPEARANCE:** Largest of the cat family. Basic color of coat ranges from white on the belly to deep yellow or orange on the back. Black stripes on the head, body, limbs, and tail; undersides mostly white. Subspecies differ in size and markings.

Silent but Deadly

Tigers are a little larger than lions. Unlike lions, which live mainly in groups, tigers live and hunt alone and have black, orange, and white striped coats. Tigers are now very rare. Only a few thousand animals survive in small pockets of rain forests. In most parts of Asia, tigers died out many years ago.

Evolution and subspecies

Tigers are thought to have evolved in Siberia, eastern Russia, two million years ago. They spread across Asia, reaching as far as the Caspian Sea and the islands of Indonesia.

Over the years, the tigers living in these different places evolved into subspecies. There were once eight

RELATIVES

The tiger is a member of the cat family, Felidae. Tigers are big cats, which belong to the genus Panthera. Other cats include:

JAGUAR (*Panthera onca*)
The jaguar is the only big cat that lives in the Americas.

LEOPARD (*Panthera pardus*)
This spotted big cat lives in forested parts of Africa and Asia.

PUMA (*Puma concolor*)
Pumas are also known as cougars or mountain lions. They live in North and South America.

CHEETAH (*Acinonyx jubatus*)
The cheetah is the fastest-running animal on Earth.

OCELOT (*Leopardus pardalis*)
A spotted small cat that ranges from Texas to Argentina in South America.

LION (*Panthera leo*)
The lion is a large, powerfully built cat. It is the second largest of the big cats. Some scientists also recognize several African subspecies, which live in different geographic regions.

LYNX (*Lynx lynx*)
Lynx and bobcats are short-tailed small cats that live in the forests of Europe, Asia, and North America.

type of tiger and the most common subspecies. It lives in India and Bangladesh. The South China tiger is slightly smaller than the Bengal tiger. There are thought to be fewer than 100 of these tigers left in the wild. The next smallest subspecies is the Malayan tiger. Despite its name, this species lives outside Malaysia, across southeast Asia. The Sumatran tiger is the smallest of all subspecies and the only one to live on an island.

SIX SUBSPECIES REMAIN:
THE BENGAL, SOUTH
CHINA, INDO-CHINESE,
SUMATRAN, AMUR,
AND MALAYAN TIGERS.

Biggest big cat
Tigers are the largest of the big cats. The other big cats are the jaguar, lion, and leopard. Big cats form a genus named *Panthera*. With a few exceptions, all other cats are small cats, which belong to around a dozen genera, including *Felis*. Small cats include bobcats, pumas, and the familiar house cat. As well as being smaller than big cats, small cats cannot roar. The structure of a bone in the throat makes that impossible.

subspecies of tigers. Now only six subspecies remain: the Bengal, South China, Indo-Chinese, Sumatran, Amur (formerly Siberian), and, recently suggested by experts, Malayan tigers. The Caspian, Javan, and Bali subspecies are now extinct.

Tigers great and small
The largest tigers live in Russia and India. An adult male Amur tiger, which lives in Russia and China, can be 13 feet (4 m) long and its coat is more shaggy than those of tigers living farther south. The Bengal tiger is the next largest

However, small cats can purr. Big cats can roar but cannot purr in the same way. Another difference between the two

---

ALL CATS ARE THOUGHT TO HAVE EVOLVED FROM A SMALL, PRIMITIVE CATLIKE ANIMAL CALLED *DINICTUS*.

---

groups is that big cats sit with their forelegs stretched out in front. Small cats generally tuck their legs under their chest when they are resting. All cats, big and small, are thought to have evolved from a small, primitive catlike animal called *Dinictis*, which lived about 40 million years ago.

Above: *The tiger is a top predator. It establishes a territory and hunts by stalking its prey and then ambushing it. To hunt successfully, the tiger has large, forward-facing eyes with which it can see in color, as well as excellent hearing. It has rounded ear flaps that funnel even the slightest sound into its ears. Forward-facing eyes ensure that the tiger has binocular vision: both eyes are used together to give a detailed, wide field of view and the ability to judge distances accurately.*

DID YOU KNOW?

Stabbing cats

The saber-toothed tiger, *Smilodon*, is one of the most familiar types of ancient cats. All of them are now extinct. They are known for their giant, pointed canine teeth. Despite being named a tiger, smilodons were only distantly related to modern tigers. Tigers and other big cats, such as lions and jaguars, are known as biting cats. They kill prey using their awesomely powerful jaws, crushing the neck or skull of their victims. Smilodons were stabbing cats. Their jaws were much weaker than those of modern big cats. Stabbing cats killed their prey by using their long teeth to rip great gashes in their victim's necks. The cats then let go and followed their victim until it finally bled to death.

ANATOMY: Amur tiger

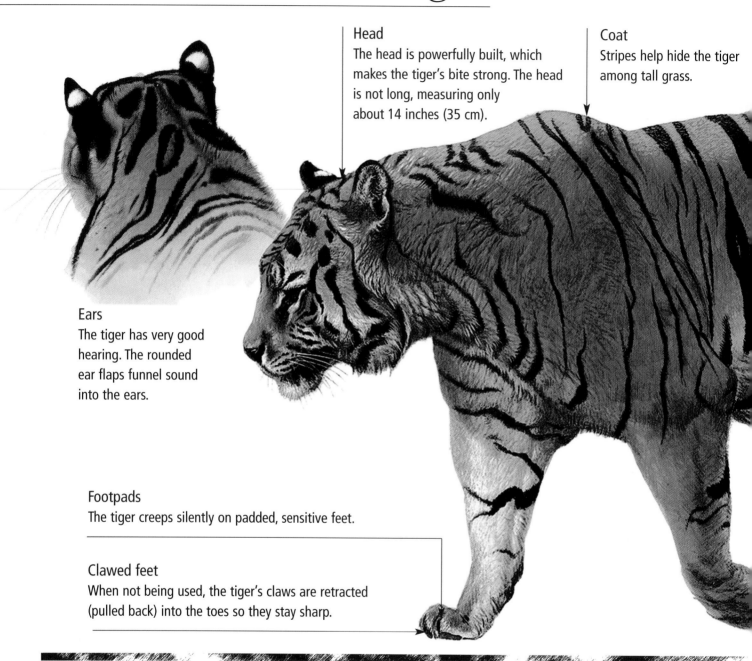

Head
The head is powerfully built, which makes the tiger's bite strong. The head is not long, measuring only about 14 inches (35 cm).

Coat
Stripes help hide the tiger among tall grass.

Ears
The tiger has very good hearing. The rounded ear flaps funnel sound into the ears.

Footpads
The tiger creeps silently on padded, sensitive feet.

Clawed feet
When not being used, the tiger's claws are retracted (pulled back) into the toes so they stay sharp.

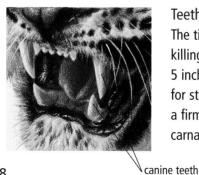

Teeth
The tiger's teeth are perfect for killing. The pointed canine teeth are 5 inches (13 cm) long. They are used for stabbing flesh, giving the bite a firm grip. Sharp cheek teeth called carnassials slice up the flesh.

canine teeth

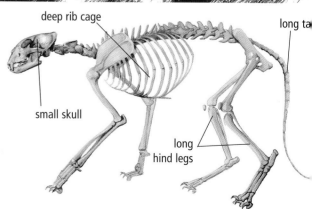

deep rib cage

long ta

long tail

small skull

long hind legs

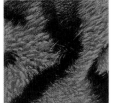

SUMATRAN

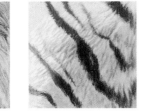

AMUR

WHITE TIGER

The largest subspecies of tiger is the Amur tiger (above right). The smallest tiger is the Sumatran tiger (above left). Female tigers are generally smaller than males.

Amur tiger

GENUS: *Panthera*
SPECIES: *tigris*
SUBSPECIES: *altaica*

SIZE

HEAD–BODY LENGTH: 106–150 inches (270–380 cm)
TAIL LENGTH: 39 inches (100 cm)
SHOULDER HEIGHT: 41–43 inches (105–110 cm)
WEIGHT: 550–675 pounds (250–306 kg)

COLORATION
Reddish golden coat with black stripes and a white underside

Bengal tiger

GENUS: *Panthera*
SPECIES: *tigris*
SUBSPECIES: *tigris*

SIZE

HEAD–BODY LENGTH: 74–87 inches (189–220 cm)
TAIL LENGTH: 32–35 inches (81–90 cm)
SHOULDER HEIGHT: 35–37 inches (90–95 cm)
WEIGHT: 400–575 pounds (180–260 kg)

COLORATION
Coat is usually fawn to orange-red with dark stripes. The fur on the belly is lighter.

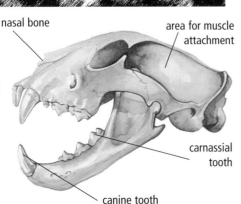

nasal bone

area for muscle attachment

carnassial tooth

canine tooth

Skeleton and skull
A tiger's skeleton is very similar to a lion's. Biologists tell the difference by looking at the nasal (nose) bones on the skull. A tiger's nasal bone is lower down than a lion's.

Grasslands, swamps, and forests

Tigers are mainly forest cats. There are three things a tiger habitat needs. First, it must have plenty of thick vegetation where the tiger can stay hidden as it stalks its prey. Second, there must be rivers or pools nearby. Tigers are good swimmers and they often cool off in deep water. The largest populations of tigers live in the swamplands of India and southeast Asia. Finally, the tiger needs to have a good supply of food. Tigers kill large animals, such as cattle, deer, and pigs.

Lone hunters

Tigers live alone and each one has a large territory of forest to itself. That territory is large enough to contain the prey needed to feed the tiger. As a result, tigers are widely spread out. Amur tigers are the most widespread, with individuals living hundreds

Left: *Padding silently out of the rain forest, this tiger is on the prowl for something to eat. Each tiger has its own territory in which it lives and hunts on its own. Tigers meet only to mate.*

Distribution

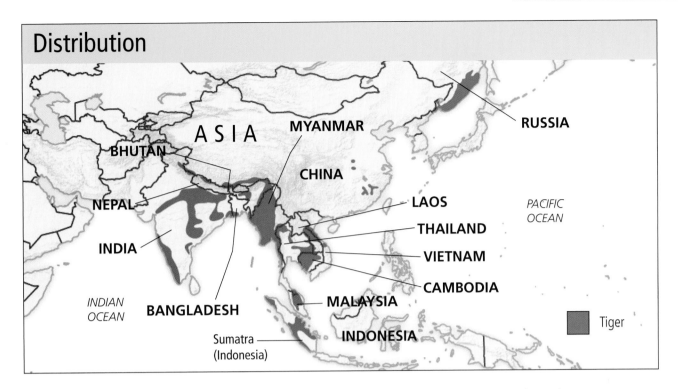

of miles apart. This is because Siberian forests in Russia are very cold and the tiger's prey are also widely spread. Amur tigers survive the cold by growing a 2-inch (5 cm) thick layer of fat under the skin.

Tigers and trees

Despite being forest hunters, tigers never climb trees to find food. Another big cat, the leopard, lives in many of the same habitats as the tiger. Leopards are excellent climbers and often leap down onto their prey from the treetops. Tigers are too heavy to climb very high, however, and they cannot compete with leopards in the trees. As a result tigers hunt on the ground.

Danger from dogs

Tigers only climb trees if they are under attack by dholes, fierce wild dogs that hunt in large packs. A tiger is much larger and stronger than a dhole. One blow from a tiger's paw would smash a dhole's skull. However, a tiger cannot fight a pack of 30 dholes at once, so it climbs into the trees for safety. Dhole packs are especially likely to attack a vulnerable female tiger when she is with her cubs.

DID YOU KNOW?

Sundarbans Tiger Reserve

The largest population of tigers in the world lives in the Sundarbans National Park. This park is in eastern India, close to the border with Bangladesh. The park includes some of the largest mangrove forest in the world. The forest grows on a huge area of islands, creeks, and swamps that forms at the mouth of the Ganges River as it empties into the Bay of Bengal.

Despite being home to the largest tiger population, the Sundarbans reserve has just 250 Bengal tigers. The region is often flooded, which makes it hard for tourists and game wardens to monitor the tigers. However, the floods also keep out the poachers.

Territorial tigers

Tigers are usually hard to find because they are rarely on the move. They spend most of their time resting in a hidden den and come out only when it safe to do so or when they are hunting prey at night.

When a tiger is out in the open, its orange coat and stripes make it stand out and the animal is very easy to see. However, tigers rarely come out into the open. When they are moving through tall grass or lying in wait in a bamboo thicket, their black stripes provide excellent camouflage, enabling them to blend into the background.

However, the cats leave several signs to show that they have been around. A tiger defends a large area of forest, called its territory. It marks the boundaries of this territory and several places within it in three ways: by scratching, spraying urine, and leaving behind feces. Tigers gouge deep scratches on tree trunks and even on rocks with their immense claws. This scratching also keeps the tiger's claws

A MALE TIGER USUALLY LETS A FEMALE PASS THROUGH ITS TERRITORY BUT CHASES AWAY MALES.

sharp. Tigers also spray urine onto bushes and tree trunks. The urine is mixed with a liquid produced by a gland under the tail. The liquid carries the tiger's unique scent. The final marks are piles of feces left in places where they

are easily seen. The feces also carry the tiger's odor.

When two tigers meet, they smell each other. The tiger with the scent that matches the scent markings is recognized as the territory owner. Males mark their territories more than females. A male tiger usually lets a female pass through its territory but chases away males.

AMAZING FACTS

- A tiger's roar can be heard 1.5 miles (2.4 km) away.
- At night, a tiger's sense of sight is six times better than a person's.
- If porcupine quills get stuck in a tiger's paw, it becomes very painful. With sore feet, the tiger cannot hunt and may even starve to death.

Above: A tiger sits among the lush vegetation of its forest home. Each tiger has its own territory and marks it by spraying urine on tree trunks, boulders, and other objects. Tigers also scratch rocks and tree trunks and leave behind piles of feces to warn other tigers not to enter an occupied area.

DID YOU KNOW?

Swimming tigers

Most cats avoid getting into water, but tigers are different. They take every chance to go for a swim because it helps them keep cool in the heat of the rain forest. They can even carry their dead prey across water. They swim in both rivers and the sea. They are strong swimmers and have been known to swim around 4 miles (6 km). On rare occasions, tigers have even killed fishers sleeping in small boats anchored a short way from the shore.

Lone hunters

Tigers hunt alone. They use their sharp senses of sight, hearing, and smell to find their prey among the thick forests. Tigers have huge appetites and eat about 4.5 tons (4 metric tons) of meat in a year. The cats prefer to prey on large animals, and their victims are often larger than themselves. Their main prey are pigs, deer, and cattle, but tigers also prey on monkeys and small rhinoceroses.

Tigers are formidable killing machines. However, only 1 in 20 hunting attempts is successful. Once a tiger has found a victim, it creeps toward it through the plant

PREY

Tigers are at the top of the food chain. They may eat fish and reptiles but generally prey on large mammals such as:

WILD BOAR (*Sus scrofa*) ▶
Tigers often prey on wild pigs by stalking them in the forests.

JAVAN RHINOCEROS (*Rhinoceros sondaicus*) ▶
Small rhinoceroses live in the forests of Asia. Tigers attack only old, sick, or young rhinoceroses.

WATER BUFFALO (*Bubalus arnee*)
Buffaloes are large plant eaters. They are armed with long horns and can fight off a tiger. Tigers often suffocate buffaloes to avoid their horns.

GAUR (*Bos gaurus*) ▶
Wild cattle, such as gaur, are among the favorite prey of tigers.

DEER AND ANTELOPE (families Cervidae and Bovidae) ▶
Tigers prey on deer and small antelope, ambushing them before they have time to sprint away.

cover. When the tiger is as close as possible, it crouches down and watches its prey, waiting for a good time to spring. When the prey comes within striking range, the tiger launches itself out of its hiding place. Within one or two bounds, the tiger pounces on its victim, using its great weight to knock the prey to the ground. The tiger stuns its victim with a blow from its mighty forepaws and then sinks its teeth into the back of the neck. The hugely strong tiger then wrenches its victim's head back. That action snaps the

1 OUT OF SIGHT: Camouflaged in the long grass, the tiger can creep up on its prey.

2 THE CHARGE: Leaping out from its hiding place, the tiger bounds toward the startled deer.

DID YOU KNOW?

Human prey

Tigers are shy animals and generally stay away from people. However, a tiger will attack a person if it feels in danger, especially when it is looking after cubs. On rare occasions tigers hunt people to eat. Most man-eating tigers, as they are called, are old or ill and cannot hunt for their normal prey. Instead they choose an easier option—humans.

prey's neck and quickly kills it. Sometimes tigers suffocate a large victim by biting its throat and holding on until the prey stops breathing.

The tiger drags its meal to a hiding place before it starts to eat, beginning with the victim's hindquarters. The cat rips flesh off the body using its sharp teeth and strips the flesh from the bones by licking with its rough tongue.

3 THE LEAP: The tiger jumps on the deer's back and bites it on the back of the neck.

4 THE BITE: The weight of the tiger knocks over the deer, and the cat kills it by breaking its neck.

185

Secret mates

A female tiger breeds once every two or three years. Each time, she is ready to mate only for a few days. She attracts males with changes in her scent. A male catching this scent tracks the female, calling to her with ear-splitting roars. The female roars back, and the pair meet in the undergrowth.

Once the two tigers meet, they smell each other. They do not simply sniff the air; they also stick out their tongues and curl up their lips into a snarl-like expression, called the flehmen response. That helps them smell their partner more deeply.

No one has ever seen tigers mating in the wild but they have often heard them. The female roars, while the male produces high-pitched squeaks. The pair mate around 20 or 30 times a day and may stay together for up to five days.

Bengal tiger

MATING SEASON: Usually in spring

GESTATION: 95–112 days

LITTER SIZE: 2–4 cubs

WEIGHT AT BIRTH: 33–42 ounces (925–1,195 g)

EYES OPEN: 10–14 days

FIRST LEAVES DEN: 2 months

INDEPENDENCE: 2 years

SEXUAL MATURITY: 3–4 years

LIFE SPAN: 15 years

Amur tiger

MATING SEASON: At any time

GESTATION: 95–112 days

LITTER SIZE: Up to 6 cubs

WEIGHT AT BIRTH: 28–53 ounces (785–1,500 g)

EYES OPEN: 10–15 days

FIRST SOLID FOOD: 14 days

INDEPENDENCE: 2–3 years

SEXUAL MATURITY: 3–5 years

LIFE SPAN: 15 years

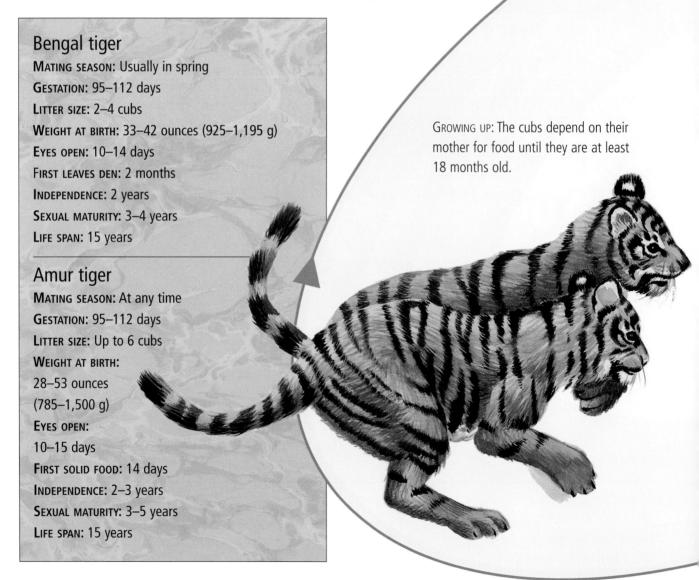

GROWING UP: The cubs depend on their mother for food until they are at least 18 months old.

Hunting during pregnancy

After mating, the male leaves and has nothing more to do with the female and their cubs. The female tiger, or tigress, is pregnant for around 100 days. She hunts right up until she is ready to give birth. The tigress gives birth at night, producing up to six cubs. Only one or two of these newborns will survive long enough to breed.

THE CUBS ARRIVE: After mating, the female tiger is pregnant for around 103 days before her cubs are born. There are usually two to four cubs, and the female raises them alone.

The life of a tiger

MOVING TIME: If the family has to move to a new den, the mother carries the cubs in her mouth.

From milk to meat

The tigress stays with the cubs for one week. At that point, the cubs eyes open. Their mother leaves the cubs to hunt but stays away for just a few hours. The cubs spend most of the next five months suckling their mother's milk. However, after one month, the cubs also begin to eat meat. That food is brought back up partly digested from the mother's stomach. At the age of around three months, the cubs are served raw meat, carried back from a kill by their mother.

From the age of six months, the cubs eat only meat. They begin to follow their mother on hunting trips and learn what to do by watching her.

Tiger cubs stay with their mother for at least two years, although Amur tiger cubs remain longer. Once the cubs leave, the tigress is able to breed again.

A dying breed?

Tigers are now very rare and one subspecies is nearly extinct. They have been shot as dangerous pests and killers, hunted for their fur, meat, and bones, and their forest habitat has been steadily cut down so the cats now have only a few places left to live. During the twentieth century the number of tigers living in the wild fell from 100,000 to about 5,000.

Most wild tigers now live in protected reserves, but their numbers are still going down. Many conservationists think that tigers will soon be extinct in the wild if more is not done to protect them. Perhaps one day, the only tigers left in the world will live in zoos.

Until about 250 years ago, people kept out of the way of tigers. In fights between a human and a tiger, the tiger usually won. However, when accurate rifles were invented, people began to kill more tigers. Rich Europeans traveled to India to hunt the greatest cat of all, and tiger skins and teeth became popular trophies.

However, most tigers were killed by farmers who had cut down the forest to make way for fields. With nowhere else to hunt, tigers began to prey on farm animals and even people. As a result, the tigers were shot.

In 1972, hunting tigers and trading in any tiger products were made illegal. However, farmers still kill tigers, even those living in reserves, to make way for more fields. Poaching (illegal hunting) is also a problem.

Down and almost out

Tigers once roamed throughout Asia. At the beginning of the twentieth century, there were more than 100,000 tigers in the wild. They lived as far west as Iran and the Caspian Sea. Tigers also lived as far south as

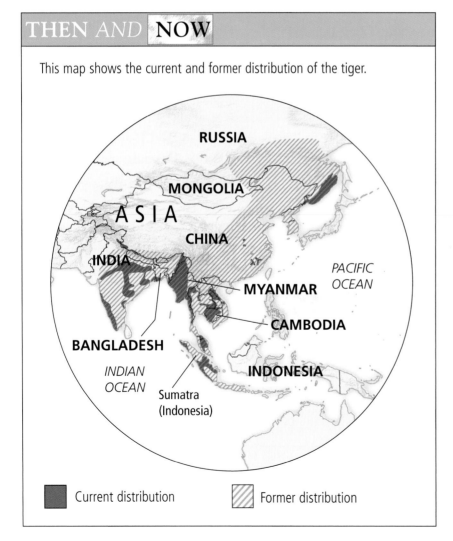

THEN AND NOW

This map shows the current and former distribution of the tiger.

RUSSIA

MONGOLIA

ASIA

CHINA

INDIA

MYANMAR

PACIFIC OCEAN

CAMBODIA

BANGLADESH

INDIAN OCEAN

INDONESIA

Sumatra (Indonesia)

■ Current distribution

▨ Former distribution

# DID YOU KNOW?

Superstitious stories

Many people in Asia believe that tigers have magical powers. Tiger meat, bones, and even whiskers are used to make potions and medicines. In Taiwan, powdered tiger bone is mixed into wine. Anyone who drinks it is said to become incredibly strong. In Malaysia, people add tiger whiskers to the food of their enemies. They believe the whiskers will kill whoever eats them. People pay a high price for pieces of a tiger's body. It is illegal to trade in tigers, but poachers can become very rich by killing tigers.

At risk

This chart shows how the International Union for the Conservation of Nature (IUCN) classifies tigers:

SOUTH CHINA TIGER	*Critically endangered*
AMUR TIGER	*Critically endangered*
SUMATRAN TIGER	*Critically endangered*
BENGAL TIGER	*Endangered*

Critically endangered means that this species faces an extremely high risk of extinction in the wild. *Endangered* means that this species faces a very high risk of extinction in the wild.

the island of Bali in Indonesia. Now there are just a few thousand tigers in the wild. It is hard to count exactly how many because tigers are so hard to find. Caspian tigers are extinct and no tigers now live on Bali or Java either. There are around 4,000 Bengal tigers in India, 1,500 Indo-Chinese tigers, and 400 to 500 of both Sumatran and Amur tigers. South China tigers number only around 30 to 80 animals.

CHECK THESE OUT

RELATIVES: • Cheetahs • Jaguars • Leopards • Lions • Lynx and wildcats
PREY: • Cattle • Deer • Pigs • Rhinoceroses

Below: *An Amur tiger leaps through the snow. Like many other creatures, these critically endangered animals face several threats, including illegal poaching, loss of habitat, and a reduction in available prey. As the human population grows, the tiger's habitat becomes smaller and splits up, making the tigers even more likely to become extinct.*

WOLVES

Fairytales and horror stories paint an unfair picture of the wolf. Often portrayed as ruthless predators of people, wolves are highly intelligent and sociable animals that go to great lengths to avoid human contact.

Above: *The gray wolf is a sleek, lean, hunting machine, with large ears, forward-facing eyes, and excellent senses of hearing, sight, and smell. It has long, rangy legs that help it travel at great speed to chase after prey and long, sharp canine teeth that secure and kill it.*

Left: *A wolf throws back its head and howls. Pack wolves generally use this form of communication to tell other wolves of the pack's presence. In this way, conflict over prey and territory is usually avoided. Wolves also communicate using a wide range of other noises, from barks and growls to whines and yelps.*

Big Bad Wolf?

Wolves are members of the dog family Canidae. Zoologists recognize two wolf species: the gray wolf (*Canis lupus*) and the red wolf (*Canis rufus*). Close relatives in the genus *Canis* include the coyote, dingo, jackal, and the familiar domestic dog breeds. All domestic breeds of dog, from the labrador to the poodle, are descended from the wolf.

Friend or foe?

The domestic dog has formed a close association with humans, but the wolf does not share in this affectionate relationship. Wolf attacks on livestock cause conflict, and mythical tales of werewolves and "the big bad wolf" of children's fairytales have only added to the animosity.

Common characteristics

Like all canids, wolves are built for hunting. They rely on their acute senses of hearing and smell to track down prey. Long legs and sleek, muscular bodies help these predators run for many miles in pursuit of prey. Wolves also have powerful jaw muscles to crunch through bone and tear through flesh.

Above: *Although some wolves live alone, most live in social groups of around 5 or 6 individuals, called packs, and packs of up to 30 are known.*

RELATIVES

There are 36 species and 13 genera within the dog family Canidae. Wolves make up 2 of 8 species from the genus *Canis*. Species from other genera include:

AFRICAN WILD DOG (*Lycaon pictus*)
As the name suggests, African wild dogs roam through the varied landscape of continental Africa, from the Sahara desert south to South Africa. Like many doglike carnivores, African wild dogs live in packs led by a dominant male and female pair.

DHOLE (*Cuon alpinus*)
Dholes are the Asian equivalent of the African wild dog. Living in packs of up to 15 individuals, dholes hunt together and take collective responsibility for the care of the offspring.

RED FOX (*Vulpes vulpes*)
The red fox is only one of a number of fox species in the dog family. Along with the gray wolf, the red fox is one of the most widely distributed land mammals in the world.

Special characteristics

At first glance, wolves look much like some domestic breeds of dogs, such as the German shepherd. However, there are many obvious differences. In general, wolves are broader and stronger, with a wide head and slanting eyes. The fur is dense and long and offers excellent protection in cold weather, owing to an insulating layer of soft underfur. This soft fur underlies the outer guard hairs, which repel water and prevent the underfur from

PRESENT-DAY DOMESTIC DOGS ARE DESCENDED FROM THE WOLF AND ARE REGARDED AS A SUBSPECIES.

becoming wet. Extra hair on the cheeks and neck make the wolf's head look even bigger to ward off rivals or enemies. Hairs on the back of a wolf's neck stand up when the wolf is threatened to make the animal look more imposing.

Wolf subspecies

There are at least 12 subspecies of gray wolves, including the common wolf from the forests of Europe and Asia and the steppe wolf from the grasslands (steppes) of central Asia.

In general, most wolves have pale undersides and darker upper parts, but the color of the fur varies among subspecies. Tundra wolves and Arctic wolves have pale or even white fur to blend in with the snow cover, but the Mexican wolf is much darker.

Present-day domestic dogs are descended from the wolf and are regarded as a subspecies. A domestic dog's scientific name is *Canis lupus familiaris*.

Family tree

Experts think that present-day canids descend from members of a family called Miacoidea, which lived during a period of time called the Eocene epoch, between 58 and 37 million years ago.

These early carnivores lived in the treetops and were much smaller than modern wolves. Gradually, they adapted to chasing prey on the ground. The earliest wolflike carnivore, known as the dire wolf, lived in the Pleistocene period, around 2 million years ago.

Above: The red wolf is smaller than the gray wolf. Once thought to be extinct in its native forest or coastal plains habitat in the southeastern United States, it has been successfully reintroduced to the wild, where scientists are following its progress.

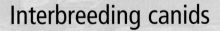

DID YOU KNOW❓

Interbreeding canids

Interbreeding is common among canids. In North America, coyotes, wolves, and domestic dogs have paired up to produce a range of hybrid animals, which are all able to breed among themselves. Some zoologists think that the red wolf is not a true species but a result of interbreeding between the gray wolf and the coyote (see *Volume 4: pages 302–317*).

Above: The gray wolf is sometimes called the timber wolf or white wolf. The many subspecies of gray wolves have various coat colors, often depending on their geographical location. For example, the tundra wolf has a pale coat that blends in with its surroundings.

ANATOMY: Gray wolf

Body shape
The wolf has a lean, tapering body and narrow chest, providing a streamlined shape as it chases after prey.

Ears
The wolf can detect faint sounds from a distance using its long, pointed ears.

Sense of smell
Like all dogs, the wolf has an acute sense of smell, which it uses to track prey and recognize other wolves and their territory.

Movement
Wolves trot as they walk, leaving a single line of paw prints. There are four toes on each hind paw and five toes on each forepaw. The wolf often spreads out its toes to grip on slippery and uneven surfaces. Large claws also help grip and are used for digging when burying food. Wolves cover vast distances in their search for food and run with great stamina using their long, slim limbs.

HIND FOOT

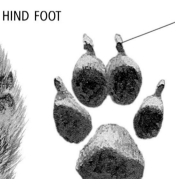

claw visible in wolf's footprint

Skeleton
The skeleton is built for speed and strength. The wrist bones (far right) are fused for extra strength.

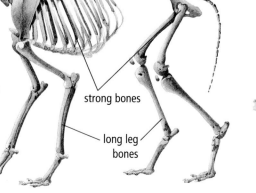

strong bones

long leg bones

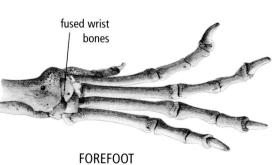

fused wrist bones

FOREFOOT

Fur

A dense layer of soft fur grows next to the skin to keep the wolf warm and dry. An outer layer of long guard hairs repels snow and water, maintaining the insulating quality of the underfur. The color of the fur varies according to range. Blotchy markings cover the head, body, and tail, helping the wolf blend in with its surroundings as it hunts.

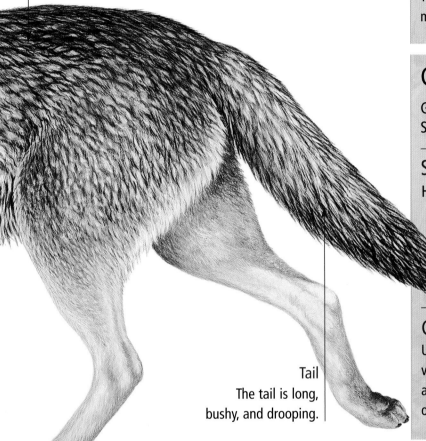

FACT FILE

The gray wolf (above right) is much larger than most domestic dogs (above left).

Gray wolf

GENUS: *Canis*
SPECIES: *lupus*

SIZE

HEAD–BODY LENGTH: 40–60 inches (100–150 cm)
TAIL LENGTH: Up to 20 inches (50 cm)
ADULT WEIGHT: Male weighs 60–150 pounds (27–68 kg); female weighs around 11 pounds (5 kg) less than the male
WEIGHT AT BIRTH: 1 pound (0.5 kg)

COLORATION

Usually gray to yellowish brown, but the color varies from white to sandy red or brown to black, according to range. Cubs have sooty brown fur or light blue to slate coloration in the Arctic.

Tail

The tail is long, bushy, and drooping.

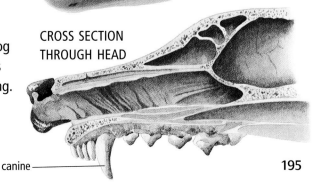

SIDE VIEW

powerful jaws

long, narrow skull

CROSS SECTION THROUGH HEAD

canine

Skull and teeth

The long, broad muzzle of the gray wolf is typical of members of the dog family Canidae. The pointed canines may reach up to 2 inches (5 cm) long. The powerful jaw muscles keep the teeth locked together, helping the wolf grip struggling prey.

Wolves of the north

The gray wolf lives in the northern hemisphere. Once common over much of northern Asia, Europe, and North America, the gray wolf is now limited to isolated populations within its former range. It is an adaptable predator, equally at home in the arctic tundra or semidesert.

Taiga and tundra

Wolves thrive in the great conifer forests, or taiga, of North America and Europe. The conifer forests provide cover, and there is plenty of fresh meat in the form of deer, elk, and moose. Farther north in the arctic tundra of Alaska,

Canada, Scandinavia, and Siberia, the winters are longer and much colder. Wolves there rely on a long, thick coat as protection from the extreme cold. The fur is pale or white and blends in well with the snow cover, making them less visible to rival wolves or prey. During the short summer, when the snow cover melts, the fur changes back to gray.

Scrublands and semideserts

Farther south, wolves roam over rocky scrublands, mountains, and sunbaked semideserts. The temperature is warm during the day and much cooler at night. In the semideserts of the Middle East

and southernmost North America, wolves tend to have short, pale or sandy-colored fur and prey on smaller mammals, such as rodents. Across most parts of Europe, wolves usually live in mountain ranges and remote woods.

Below: *This wolf is howling either to locate fellow pack members or reveal its presence to neighboring packs.*

DID YOU KNOW?

Wolves on the up

Following centuries of persecution by humans, European wolves have staged a minor comeback in many parts of Europe. In Italy, there is now a population of more than 500 wolves compared with fewer than 100 individuals in the 1970s. This expanding Italian population has migrated north through the Alps to France, Germany, and Switzerland. Wolves in Scandinavia have also fared much better. Wolves from northern Finland have migrated south to repopulate Norway and Sweden, which had no native wolves in the early 1970s.

Distribution

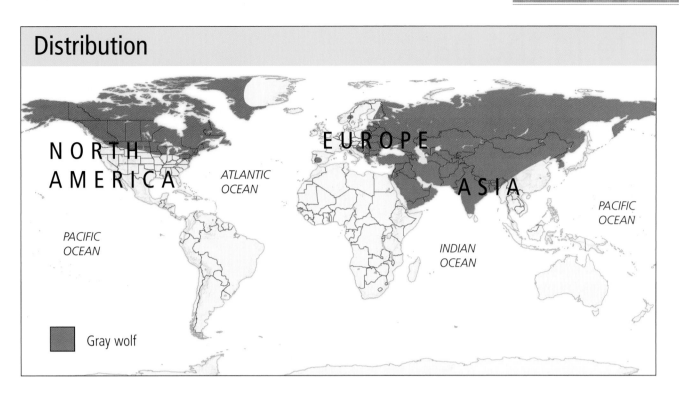

Gray wolf

Life in the pack

Most wolves live in highly organized groups called packs. Each member of the pack works as part of a team, living and hunting together and fiercely protecting the territory from neighboring packs. Each pack usually includes five or six individuals, although pairs are common and larger packs of up to 30 wolves have been recorded.

Pack mentality

There is an obvious hierarchy within the pack. A dominant male and female, called the alpha pair, lead the pack. They are the only wolves in the pack to breed, and they mate for life. They are usually the parents of the other pack members. Below the alpha pair come the beta

1 HARMONY: An adult wolf stays relaxed as younger pack members play-fight and jostle for status. Each wolf knows its place in the hierarchy, and serious conflicts are rare.

2 SUBMISSION: A lower-ranking wolf rolls onto its back and flattens its ears as a sign of submission.

3 FACIAL EXPRESSIONS: The facial expressions of wolves reveal a great deal about their feelings. The subtle interactions between wolves are often invisible to outsiders.

UNDER THREAT: A wolf under threat or feeling insecure may flatten its ears and hide its teeth to indicate fear or submission.

PROTRUDING TONGUE: A protruding tongue may be a sign of submission. However, here the wolf's erect ears indicate hostility.

STRONG DOMINANCE: A wolf with bared teeth, erect ears, and staring eyes is communicating all the signs of strong aggression.

PRICKED-UP EARS: Pricked-up ears indicate confidence, but the tight-lipped "grin" shows that the wolf is not sure of itself.

male and female, and so on through to the subadult wolves and old or sick individuals at the bottom of the pack. Most of the adults take part in hunting expeditions, but some stay behind to act as helpers for the dominant pair's pups. As the younger wolves become ready to mate, some leave to start their own packs.

Pecking order and communication

A typical wolf pack remains relatively stable in terms of size and structure throughout the year. Confrontations do occur from time to time, however, especially during the breeding season.

Wolves use body language and a variety of facial expressions to settle disputes and establish dominance.

A high-ranking wolf raises his or her tail, stands with stiff legs and bare teeth, and pushes lower-ranking individuals. The lower-ranking wolf lowers his or her head, flattens the ears, and droops the tail between its legs in cowering submission.

In most cases, however, pack members are friendly toward each other. They usually greet each other by wagging their tails and licking one another's faces. Very rarely do confrontations lead to physical fights between wolves.

DID YOU KNOW ?

Territories and scent marking

A wolf pack lives in a well-defined territory, which may vary from 40 square miles (100 sq km) to more than 400 square miles (1,000 sq km) depending on the availability of prey. Wolves mark the boundaries of the territory with urine and scent from anal glands at the base of the tail. Scent marking is usually carried out by the alpha male, but other members of the pack add their own scent marks.

Boundary markers act as a deterrent to neighboring wolf packs, allowing them to live alongside each other in relative peace. Individuals from one pack who accidentally stray across unmarked regions of the boundary risk being attacked and killed by wolves from another pack. However, it is rare for one pack to invade a neighboring pack's territory. If this does occur, the attackers will head for the pack's resting place and aim to kill or scatter the defending wolves to take over the territory.

Hunters and trackers

1 HOWLING TOGETHER: A wolf pack begins to howl. This often takes place before the wolves set out to hunt. Hunting trips are rarely successful— perhaps 1 in 10 results in a kill.

DID YOU KNOW?

Wolfing down food

The saying "wolf down your food" comes from a hungry wolf's ability to eat vast quantities of meat in one sitting. A wolf may go for days without food, so when it does make a kill, it gorges as much as it can—often up to 20 pounds (9 kg) at a time.

2 FOLLOW THE LEADER: The wolf pack begins its hunting trip by walking in single file behind the alpha male.

3 TEAMWORK: Wolves usually try to pick out weak or young individuals because healthy adults can be dangerous. When the pack tackles large prey, such as a musk ox, it must hunt as a team to have any chance of success.

Wolves eat a wide range of prey. A pack of wolves prefers to hunt large mammals, such as caribou, deer, elk, and moose. Because large prey is not always available in many parts of the wolf's range, smaller animals, such as birds, rodents, and frogs, may also be hunted. Livestock and domestic dogs are also fair game where human settlements have overlapped the wolf's range. Wolves have even been known to eat flower buds, fruit, and lichens when they are particularly hungry.

Sensing prey

Wolves rely on keen senses to track their prey. A wolf can hear faint sounds over vast distances and detect a much wider range of pitch than a person can hear. The sense of smell is also excellent. A wolf can detect the smell of a moose from a distance of more than 1 mile (1.5 km). From the scent, it can figure out the condition and movements of the animal it is tracking. Wolves can smell hundreds of thousands more odors than a person can detect. They can even remember the smells of landmarks to build an scent map of their surroundings.

In for the kill

Wolves hunt large mammals in packs. The pack animals roam

PREY

Wolves usually hunt large mammals to provide enough meat for all the pack members, but they will also take smaller prey when the opportunity arises.

BEAVER (*Castor canadensis*)
Beavers are an important prey item for wolves and other large carnivores, such as coyotes, foxes, and wolverines.

CARIBOU (*Rangifer tarandus*)
Caribou (domesticated forms are called reindeer) are migratory mammals, moving to the Arctic tundra in the short summer to feed on the highly nutritious plants that grow there. Wolves take full advantage of this seasonal supply of fresh meat.

SNOWSHOE HARE (*Lepus americanus*)
The white winter coat of the snowshoe hare blends in with the snow cover, making it difficult for wolves to spot them.

MOUNTAIN GOAT (*Oreamnos americanus*)
These nimble-footed mammals graze at high altitudes, evading predation by bounding across rocky mountain ledges.

MOOSE (*Alces alces*)
The moose is a formidable opponent for a pack of hungry wolves. As well as being a speedy runner and a good swimmer, a healthy adult moose may fight back and even kill attacking wolves.

4 CLOSING IN: One wolf heads off the musk ox, while the others bring it down.

in single file, sniffing out burrows and scent marking the territory. When the wolves detect the scent of prey, they move more purposefully, homing in on the target with ruthless efficiency.

Some wolves act as decoys, while the rest of the pack wait in ambush. When the prey has been startled and starts to run, the fastest runners move in for the chase.

Once the prey tires, the wolves go for the kill. A powerful bite to the neck or head is usually enough to kill the animal. The wolves then gorge themselves on as much food as they can, including bones and skin.

When they have eaten their fill, the wolves may return to feed their cubs with fresh or regurgitated meat or lie under cover until the meal is digested.

Dominance wins the day

Mating between wolves occurs between late winter and early spring. Only the dominant pair mates, and tensions run high as they defend their position within the pack. Once the pecking order is settled, the dominant pair mate. Mating takes place two or three times a day for up to 14 days.

Six weeks after mating, the pregnant female builds a den in loose soil close to a river or lake. The burrow is around 16 inches (40 cm) high and 26 inches (65 cm) wide. The female gives birth to her litter in this secure den nine weeks after mating. There are usually five or six pups in a litter, and they are blind, deaf, and entirely dependent. The pups can see and hear around two to three weeks after birth. A week or two later, they take their first

steps outside the den to play. Although only one pair of wolves breeds, all the adults take responsibility for the care of the pups.

The female sleeps in a rounded hollow about 6 feet (1.8 m) from the den's entrance. The pups sleep in a snug chamber 6 feet farther along

GROWING UP: The young wolves establish a social structure through play-fights. These skirmishes lay the foundations for their future role in the pack.

Gray wolf

GESTATION: 63 days

LITTER SIZE: 5–6 pups

WEIGHT AT BIRTH: 1 pound (450 g)

EYES OPEN: 2–3 weeks

WEANED: 7–8 weeks

LEAVE THE DEN: Up to 10 weeks

HIERARCHY: Dominant pup becomes apparent after 12 weeks

FOLLOW THE PACK: At 3–5 months

INDEPENDENCE: 10 months

FULLY GROWN: 18 months

SEXUALLY MATURE: Female 2 years; male 3 years

LIFE SPAN: Up to 16 years in the wild; 20 years for captive individuals

from their mother's sleeping hollow. The pups emerge from the den for the first time after around four or five weeks. After 8 to 10 weeks, mother and pups abandon the den and establish a summer meeting place. The young wolves can play safely here, while the mature wolves move back and forth on hunting trips. At 10 months of age, a wolf may join in on a hunting expedition for the first time.

Adult life

By 18 months, a wolf reaches full adult size. Most female wolves are not ready to mate until they are two years old; males are not ready until they are three. At this point, the mature wolves may abandon the pack and find a mate.

In the wild, a wolf usually lives to the age of 10. A few individuals live longer if they are fed and protected by younger members of the pack. In most cases, however, old and sick wolves are cast out from the pack and left to die.

INDEPENDENCE: The wolves reach sexual maturity in their second or third year. Some individuals may leave the pack to mate and claim their own territory.

The life of a wolf

SECURE DEN: After the alpha male and female mate in late winter or early spring, the female gives birth around nine weeks later to a litter of five or six pups. The pups are blind, deaf, and helpless in their safe, secure den.

DEPENDENT PUPS: The pups rely on their mother for milk and protection.

Range reduction threat

There is an ongoing love-hate relationship between humans and wolves. Many farmers persecute wolves in retaliation for countless instances of wolves taking cattle and other livestock. Fairytale stories of "big, bad wolves" eating people only add to the animal's poor reputation. These direct threats from farmers and hunters are not all; the wolf's natural range is shrinking as a result of human activities, such as forest clearance and settlement. Wolves are only relatively

> MANY PEOPLE ARE WORKING HARD TO SAVE WOLF POPULATIONS.

abundant in places that are too cold for people to settle. These places include the conifer woods of North America, mainly in Canada and Alaska, as well as Siberia in Asia. Once widespread throughout Europe, only a handful of wolf populations survive in Scandinavia, Italy, Spain, and Portugal.

Conservation efforts

Many people are working hard to save wolf populations. In the United States, the Endangered Species Act protects wolves. In Canada, wolves are fully protected in national parks and nature reserves. Regulated culls (legal killings) are permitted in situations where the wolf is considered to threaten

THEN AND NOW

This map shows the current and former distribution of the gray wolf.

GREENLAND

EUROPE

NORTH AMERICA

ATLANTIC OCEAN

ASIA

PACIFIC OCEAN

INDIAN OCEAN

Current distribution

Former distribution

At risk

The International Union for the Conservation of Nature (IUCN) lists only the red wolf in the *Red List of Threatened Species:*

RED WOLF	*Critically endangered*

Critically endangered means that the species faces an extremely high risk of extinction in the wild in the immediate future.

Left: *The red wolf is critically endangered. Its range has been much reduced as people have spread into its habitat in the southeastern United States.*

livestock or other wild animals. In some areas of Europe farmers are compensated for animals killed by wolves.

Key to the success of these efforts is the hope that people will overcome centuries-old fears and hostility. The wolf is close to extinction in many countries. Sanctuaries need to be set aside for wolves, and their numbers carefully monitored by scientists.

CHECK THESE OUT

RELATIVES: • African wild dogs • Coyotes • Dogs • Foxes • Jackals • Red foxes
PREY: • Bison • Deer • Goats and sheep • Hares and pikas

DID YOU KNOW?

What is the red wolf?

The red wolf looks much like the gray wolf, but it has longer legs, larger ears, and shorter, reddish fur. Most zoologists accept the two types as unique species, but some now question the distinction. They believe that the red wolf might be the result of breeding between gray wolves and coyotes. Research has provided mixed results. Studies of body form and behavior support the red wolf's status as a unique species. However, genetic studies reveal a close relationship between gray wolves and coyotes. In some cases, zoologists cannot be sure whether populations previously considered to be red wolves are hybrids of red and gray wolves or of red wolves and coyotes. The dilemma has clear implications for conservation efforts for the critically endangered red wolf. In the 1980s, the U.S. Fish and Wildlife Service started a captive-breeding program to restore the North American red wolf population. If the red wolf is not a true species, the USFWS may have misdirected its efforts.

INDEX